LOLA R. MARIE

THE MINIMALIST BABE

TIDYING UP YOUR WHOLE LIFE

Cover Design: Srjdan Filipovic

Photo Credit: 1.mallmo 2.universehearsus — stock.adobe.com

ISBN 978-1-989526-05-7

VisualBee Publishing 2019

info@visualbeepublishing.com

CONTENTS

"Simplicity is the ultimate sophistication"
— Leonardo da Vinci

INTRODUCTION

The birth of this book

A few years ago, I woke up on a cold Monday morning with the best feeling.

My bedroom was moderately sized. It had a closet, a side table, a bedside light, and a bed. Nothing more. Nothing less. A single big window in the room overlooked a park with a lovely lake decorating the center of it. A few children played while their parents watched over them. It appeared to be a day like any other, yet I felt happier than before.

Outside, the sky was surprisingly clear and a brilliant shade of blue. There was a light breeze. The street was busy with people starting the week, sipping coffee, and scrolling through their phones while rushing to reach their next destination.

The buzz of moving vehicles and passers-by continued as usual, but they did not dominate or overpower the sounds of the streets surrounding me. Instead, they existed in harmony, seamlessly merging into the backdrop that made this world familiar to me. The only thing that I could hear, feel, and experience was a sense of silence and calm. The sensation echoed into the hallway, to the kitchen, and the rest of the house.

You know what? I'm really enjoying my life, I remember thinking. It was such an odd thought, but I welcomed it. The hallway was open and welcoming. One bending stair led to another and descending them helped coax my mind into alertness. The planters stood tall and beautiful; alone but still part of the entire space. They were green and fresh and full of life.

In fact, the entire house felt alive. It was as if the few things I owned had a real connection with each other and, most importantly, with me. They gave me space which metaphorically translated into clarity, but appeared to watch over me around the corner and at a distance. The doorway opened out to the bright and purposeful world that I knew. This was (and is) my world and I'm very happy with it.

I've always been this way

With my recent years being those of intense introspection, I have come to this realization; I've always erred on the side of keeping things simple. However, it was a suppressed aspect of myself I hadn't learnt to fully express yet. Years of social conditioning had squelched my inner minimalist. Following this revelation, I made the conscious decision to nurture the minimalist within me. I gave it permission to make alterations to my over-complicated life. I've tried to live my most recent years through mindful choices, and I'm happy to say that I love the way life has turned out. I've watched myself succeed over some of life's most challenging experiences with a sense of calm, and I've emerged stronger and happier than before every time.

So what was extra special about this day?

I'd invited a friend over for dinner and conversations of my travels shifted to how she always wanted to do everything that I was doing but couldn't. She spoke about her work and how disconnected she felt with it. Because she wasn't very interested or invested in her work, she felt she couldn't give it her best. That was why she often found herself spending needless extra hours every day on her tasks, dragging herself through each day to meet her responsibilities. This had really taken a toll on her personal life and mood, and in a bid to make up for that feeling, she found herself binge eating and shopping endlessly on clothes; most of which she never wore as a result of her recent weight gain.

I was worried for her. You see, I'd known her long enough to realize that this wasn't her. She was intelligent and talented and I believed she could do better for herself. It was at that point that I realized how different my story was from hers and I was glad I took the steps I did in life (which I will share with you in this book).

I really wanted her to be happy. I saw the immense potential in her and so, in my bid to help her see and do better, I lent her my ears and time. Over the next few weeks, we spoke at length. I spoke about my life choices and how, by simply accumulating less, I continue to be my happiest and most productive self every day. The intention was not to gloat about the problems I didn't have, but to show her a possible way out.

I'm delighted to tell you that my intention worked well. After weeks of talking and sharing my decisions in life, she called me last week to tell me that she'd begun to see results. She'd parted with a lot of her stuff and, therefore, had less to worry about. She'd changed jobs and was now doing something she always wanted to do: care for animals and pets. She said she was happy and felt free. She'd begun eating mindfully and was hoping to fit into the clothes she'd never worn before. She really sounded happy and I was glad — relieved even — that it had all worked out for her in the end. And with those feelings, I realized that I was finally ready to write this book.

If it worked for me and for her, I believe it can work for you too

I've always been simple-minded. However, I was a bit of a mess and I couldn't quite place my finger on what made life… well, suck. And so, over the years, I've embraced this minimalist philosophy. As a result, I have a deeper understanding of myself. I've simplified my thought process, belongings, diet, finances, health, home, and social circle. I've also taken my time to fully experience the changes that come with it. I've been this way for a while now, yet I've taken all these years to write this book.

So what took me so long?

There are a few reasons I purposefully took my time.

- I wanted to experience the shift as naturally and gradually as I could, without rushing into the 'this-is-it' feeling.
- I wanted a more sustainable change and that takes time and patience.
- I wanted to know my process was replicable. After all, why else share it?
- I wanted to wait until I felt I knew enough and that what I knew was worth sharing.
- I was so engrossed in living in the experience that I became one with it.
- I am still seeking more knowledge. There is so much to learn but I now know that I have enough to share.

You see, I did not set out to write this book. Yet here I am, privileged to share my experiences with you. In fact, none of the best experiences in my life have been planned; they all came together as if they were meant to be. They happened in the most organic way, as if to guide me to my higher purpose; that of creating a positive impact on the lives of my readers. For that, I'm ever indebted.

Why am I writing this?

I'm not one to preach. In fact, I find the act of trying to convince someone of a different lifestyle quite unnatural. Everyone has their own path in life and their own timing. I understand the principles of minimalism may not be for everyone. You may now be wondering why then have I taken the time to write this book? The thing is that I believe everyone is a minimalist at heart; we were simple at birth, after all.

I often hear others reminisce about the old days. How life was simple and vivid during childhood. Music was heavenly, the outdoors was our domain and ice cream was everything! There was an authentic nuance to life that now most of us only have access to through our memories; the bitter-sweet nostalgia.

This book is about reviving that childlike glee. It's about happiness and what it *really* takes to be happy. It's about realizing that less is more, and about letting go of your possessions and the depressions that come with it. It's about doing away with the unessential so we can concentrate on the things that are truly important to us. Finally, it's about living in the present and being ready to accept the wonderful things waiting to reach you.

Our need for more: One of society's most grave and (until now) ignored illnesses

The Minimalist Babe is about saying goodbye to the extras in life from time to time, finding happiness in having less, and finding your inner badass through your newly acquired freedom. It is the culmination of all my research; a toolbox of sorts filled with tips, techniques, exercises, and prompts that have helped me be my most authentic self.

When I'm not writing, I spend my time nurturing relationships and learning new skills. I focus on being healthy and purposeful and it's working like magic. I am in the happiest phase of my life and want the same for each one of you. This book is an attempt to manifest that vision. Let us cut out the bitter side of nostalgia and bite into the sweetness of life that is now.

Love,
Lola

PART 1 — WHY?

CHAPTER 1 — DISCOVERING YOUR AUTHENTIC SELF

"Authenticity is the daily practice of letting go of who we think we are supposed to be and embracing who we actually are." — **Brené Brown**

Jordan, a square-jawed American man could pass for a movie star. He's tall, handsome, and carries a charismatic style that makes him stand out from the crowd. He's intelligent and extremely driven. Working as an intern for a top financial service company, he puts in long hours of work and has his life cut out in front of him. He wakes up at 6 am every morning, heads out for a run, grabs a cup of coffee on his way back home, gets ready and leaves for work at 8.30 am, scrolling through some daily reads on his commute to work by train.

He spends his work hours mostly sitting in front of his computer, sometimes moving across different rooms to attend different meetings. He finishes up at around 6 pm and spends the next hour or so catching up with friends over drinks and food. He then takes the train home, during which time he listens to trending songs on iTunes and browses through the latest in tech on his phone. The latest MacBook Pro has caught his attention. A few of his friends own it and believe it's a must-have. He has been looking at different variations of the same model recently, and wondering whether he should take the plunge and purchase it. He spends his weekends relaxing, mostly watching movies, doing some shopping, or hanging out with friends and family.

Nina, a budding artist, who lives a few blocks away from Jordan, has a different yet similar lifestyle. She's beautiful, smart, and incredibly creative. She lives in a studio apartment that doubles-up as her workplace during the day. She works as a freelancer and keeps herself busy with a few projects. Being a morning person, she likes to start her day with an early morning stroll with her dog and a coffee from her favorite café. She then spends the remaining part of the day sketching and creating her designs.

Given a choice, she'd love to be by herself and isn't much of a social being. Nina's parents don't like the idea of her being alone though, and want her to socialize more often, but she has always struggled with fitting in. However, it's critical for her profession and growth of her small business that she makes an effort to mingle with people. Fortunately, Nina has managed to become a part of a social circle that she now spends time with. She spends her evenings with a gang of friends and often tries to match their sense of fashion and even how they speak and the topics they speak about so as to fit in. She doesn't earn very much but saves up to try and dress a bit like them. She also listens to the same songs. She believes they help her feel connected and relevant, and sees the positive results of her painstaking efforts unfold all around her. For example, she gets tagged with a picture of her and her friends every now and then on social media, and she enjoys how her friends believe she's the happiest person around — the perfect balance of beauty, intelligence, and creativity.

Paul, a family man with three young kids, a son and two daughters, lives in a suburban area. He's a manager at a reputable IT company that's located at the heart of the city and spends his weekdays traveling back and forth from work to home and home to work. He loves his family dearly and works hard to provide them with everything they want. They've recently bought a house and financed a new car. Dave, his eldest, wants to train for boxing. The little one, Lilly, is all ready to join school this year. Like most people with a desk job, Paul spends his workdays answering emails and attending meetings. He finishes work at 6 pm, but has to travel for over an hour to reach home. Once home, he spends time with his family, usually watching movies, doing some shopping, having dinner, and going out. Recently, the neighbors dropped by after having been on vacation. They bought Paul's family some chocolates and expressed what a wonderful time they had in Spain. Needless to say, this has got the kids all excited and they are rooting for a Spain vacation of their own this summer.

Paul is nearing his 50's and knows he has to work for another decade or so. He plans to put in extra hours over the next few months and wants to make an impression in time for the yearly appraisals. A promotion and some additional revenue will always come in handy.

When you look at them, Jordan, Nina, and Paul are three different people with different interests, but they share a somewhat similar lifestyle. The parallelism is striking to say the least. The truth is that Jordan, Nina, and Paul aren't alone. We are all like them in some way or the other. Looking around, you'll realize that we all have a lot in common. Over the years, while trying to fit in, we've created a society that looks and functions in a certain way. Everyone looks and behaves the same way. They like the same things, listen to the same music — we are all living the reflections of each other. We want to have what others have, do what others do. We want more because that's the only thing we know. Sadly, we also believe it is the only way to be.

We all started out as minimalists, so what really changed?

When you think about it, we didn't come into this world with all the pomp and glory we seek from it as we grow older. Everyone started out as a minimalist. So what really changed?

The answer is quite obvious. We changed, and as a result, society changed. Now it's got to a point where a few of us who want to reform are deemed 'unfit' and 'outlaws' simply because we don't want to subscribe to the expectations and so-called image-building process of our brotherhood.

The mirroring starts early

The reality is that it starts even before you realize you've been inducted into the process. As kids, we look at other kids playing in the playground and start to mirror the behavior of the group that has everybody's attention. We do this because we seek acceptance too. Parents are even encouraged to leave their children with other kids so as to help them with this process. One thing snowballs into another and, before we know it, the system of mimicry has become one of our traits. This trait then continues into adulthood, only getting more obsessive with time.

Is it something we constantly feed off of?

In today's world, we all experience information overload and access to that information is instantaneous. For better or worse, globalization has become a key part of our society. The majority of people live on their smartphones, staring, scrolling, and frantically searching for ways to find more attention, acceptance, and happiness.

We speak to our friends on phones, exchange notes on phones, order stuff (plenty of it) on our phones. Worse still, we've now got to a point where we seek validation by showcasing our lifestyle so as to garner likes, shares, and comments for it. If you haven't broadcasted it, then it just didn't happen. I mean, really? Sadly, most of what we do and show isn't us but a reflection of those who surround or influence us.

The general idea is to believe that if we're doing the same as everyone else, then we're right and we're accepted. We're doing good. But are we really? Does mirroring the reflection of others, even when you feel differently deep down, make you feel good? Does that even account for validation?

We alter our looks, our speech patterns, our expressions, and what we want to say depending on who we are talking to. We all want to be on the right side and so put out what we think the person in front of us thinks is right. There simply isn't any room for authenticity.

Staying true to your authentic self

Often, we end up living our lives backwards. A lot of people pursue greater rewards in order to lead the life we seek and be the person we truly believe we are. For instance, some people might pursue wealth as a means to lead a happier life, but end up doing things that contradict their inner belief systems, making them feel shortchanged and unhappy in the process. However, the way it actually works is quite the reverse. They must first be the person they believe they are (stay positive and happy despite any challenges, knowing that through it all, they'll come out successful), then do what they really need to do in order to lead the life they desire. The key is to stay true to oneself.

As E. E. Cummings once quoted, "*To be nobody-but-yourself in a world which is doing its best, night and day, to make you everybody else — means to fight the hardest battle which any human being can fight; and never stop fighting.*" Staying authentic in a way that reflects our thoughts, actions, and words is one of the most courageous battles that we'll ever fight, but it's a battle that is worth fighting for.

Tapping into your core and basics: Who are you at your simplest and minimalist self?

Dig deep and look at yourself. What do you see? What are the essential things that define you, without which you truly feel incomplete? What do you need to experience these basic things?

You see, Minimalism doesn't mean becoming 'culty', boring, or being cheap to prove a point. There are no set rules to define a minimalist. So you don't have to knock out stuff from your list simply because it's large or expensive by virtue of its size or cost. It's not like you're certified a minimalist simply because everything you own can fit into a bag. Minimalism is about living life with only the things that are truly essential for you. It is about only accumulating things that are important to you and letting go of those that are not. It's about finding the freedom to truly live by making some overdue cuts.

Minimalism is a way of life

Life is all about changes and evolution. As we age, our beliefs change, and with it so do our priorities and needs. Things that are important will vary. With experience, the accumulation and reduction will also vary. As you start living a minimalist life, you'll find new methods of living a more authentic and simple life. That's the beauty of it — you will learn something new every day. You will realize a simpler way of living. Every morning, you will wake up to the idea of experiencing that simplicity. Minimalism is a prologue for shaping your own unique story and you have a lifetime to discover it. The feeling is extremely liberating to say the least.

Points to remember

- We all started out as minimalists. So what changed?
- Mirroring starts early. Are there any aspects of society you find yourself mimicking?
- Life is about changes and evolution. So how far have you evolved?
- Tap into your authentic self. Who are you at your simplest and most minimalist self?

CHALLENGE TIME

- Do something each day that reflects your deepest needs, wishes, and values.

CHAPTER 2 — TRIMMING THE EXTRAS

"You create more space in your life when you turn your excess baggage to garbage." — ***Chinonye J. Chidolue***

We were simple at birth. So, what happened? Take a moment to delve into your past. What beneficial behavioral patterns have been lost with time? What did your minimalism as a child look like? For example, I loved collecting things but I was never a hoarder. There was never more than or two of anything, and each item was a 'special treasure' that had to be kept safe and cherished. I never asked for more and didn't spend my allowance on every piece of Spice Girls merchandise. Instead, I remember being happy with what I had and used my first earnings from my newspaper route mindfully, even putting a tiny bit of it in my savings, which was a tin milk can in which I had punctured a coin slot with a knife. Although my childhood wasn't as ideal as I would have liked it to be, I can't remember a time when I felt truly deprived. As a family, we were always tight-knit. My parents gave us everything we needed, which was traditional family values. This would be the springboard we would use to grow into self-sufficient humans, capable of acquiring what we wanted. There was love, togetherness, great times, and plenty of great conversations. I believe it is what shaped me to be the way I am and I'm very grateful for that. This fostering of inner resourcefulness combatted any type of boredom that came my way. As an adult, I can't remember the last time I was bored, save for the times I felt obligated to do something, i.e., sit through boring lectures (cough cough).

As I grew up, innate minimalism became a thing of the past, I had been socialized like the rest of us into the 'real world'. I became more and more aware of what I lacked instead of what I really needed. It wasn't something that I constantly thought about, but something that guided my purchasing decisions almost subconsciously. However, consciously, I mostly knew what mattered and what didn't, what was a time waster and what was worth my time. This didn't do much to help the subconscious program of 'lack' running my life.

Part of my evolution: Knowing what I have and what I want

During our formative years we never truly want more than what we already have. We are content. For example, we make do with the Barbie doll with only one leg and its hair half-shaved off. When we do want more, most of the time it comes from juvenile insecurity and the social pressures of fitting in. Repeat these instances multiple times throughout the years and the result is an ingrained habit of giving in to this sense of lack. Overcoming this habit takes conscious thought and deliberate action.

For instance, soon after I completed my degree, I felt the pressure of proving my education wasn't useless. I saw my peers buying new cars, a few buying houses, and others making big purchases that I didn't feel made sense for people in their early 20s. While I did deliberate on whether or not I should follow their path for a brief moment, my better judgment overrode the sense of inadequacy I felt by looking at other people's lives.

Somehow, I knew that what they were doing would come back to haunt them and I didn't want to go down that lane. Instead, I did what made sense to me. I returned to my parents' home, and bought a total beater; you know the kind that would take me to work and back. I also saved up a bit from every paycheck and spent mindfully. In fact, the only large purchases I made were on travel tickets, and that in my mind was very much worth it. I place more importance on life experiences than material needs and, therefore, spend my money traveling to places I've never been to, each time discovering a little more of me while learning something new about a place, its people, and culture.

When what you own defines how happy you think you can be

Here's the thing — I can be what people term as 'extra', but I also have a side of me that thrives off of common sense. And the Common Sense Lola almost always outsmarts the Extra Lola. For example, while at university, I lived with a friend in a moderately-sized apartment. It had a nice leather couch, a spacious living room, a kitchen, a pantry (yes, that too), and two bedrooms. More than enough for two students you'd think. But it wasn't. It so happened that I met the person who lived on the topmost floor of the building and he told me about the wonderful views from his apartment. Suddenly Extra Lola wanted to experience that. I remember wondering about it frequently, going on about it, and even pining for it. It was always a sense of what we already had not being good enough and feeling like we could do better. I would constantly remind myself that we don't have a high-rise view or a terrace where we could have barbeques (seriously? I mean, we were students with very little time to study let alone socialize, and even less money to spend on fancy barbeques).

Suddenly, the home that gave us so many wonderful memories seemed less worthy. It was good alright, but not great. And I could do with great. Needless to say, Common Sense Lola won. The thought of eating instant noodles every day in an epic top-floor apartment didn't jive.

It's the same with a lot of people. It might be different things for different people, but most people dive into the thought of needing more. It's the unheard narrative that's ringing in most minds. While it's okay to indulge in things that bring value to your life, I believe it's a worthless chase to run after things simply because you believe it will give you the validation of status and image. What's not so right is when you buy stuff out of habit, even when you don't really need them and might never really use them, but still buy them simply out of an urge. That attitude needs to change and I'm here to help you through it.

When what you have is never enough

Take our jobs, for example. Clearly you wanted to work where you are currently posted at some point in time. You wouldn't have got the job had you not applied for it, sat through the screenings, and given it your best. It may or may not have been your number one choice or the industry that you really wanted to get into, but that doesn't dismiss the point that you needed a job and wanted this job when you applied for it. No doubt that some part of you was even happy when you got it. So what's changed? Where is that happiness? Why do you feel shortchanged? Why do you keep wondering what a career change might be like?

The same goes for our belongings. Let's look inside our wardrobes for a minute. Let's admit that there have been times when some of us have spent our weekends shopping for things to wear. Some of us select most of what we buy and do so because we like them the most from the choices presented. So why do we always feel like we don't have anything decent enough to wear? Why is it always, "Oh, but I've worn this before/I'm too fat/I'm too slim for this now/this is so outdated?" What happened from the time you first bought it to now? Why don't you have the same level of excitement? Where did your happiness go?

Smartphones, living spaces, clothes, jewelry, TV...the list can go on. Sadly, there is no end to it.

We get used to things

Buying everything that you want or think that you need can sometimes desensitize you to a point when you no longer feel good about buying them. Think about something you loved to wear. Do you share the same level of love and excitement for it? Probably not. The grandeur of the purchase tends to wear off with time and use. You eventually get used to the idea of having your wishes fulfilled and start taking things for granted. And when that happens, you get bored of the things you have and seek something more and new. Sadly, this is a never-ending pattern that almost always leads to unhappiness unless you do something about it.

Dependency on the things we buy

Some people can become dependent on the things they buy and cannot function without them. What might have started out to be occasional becomes routine. When that happens, they get used to the idea of having things presented in a certain way — so much so that their brain begins to recognize the sequence of events or visuals as a stimulus to do something. When indulgence becomes dependency, it becomes more than a necessity. It becomes obsessiveness. Now, team this with your nature to get bored of things and your habit to buy new things and visualize how detrimental things could get. The enormous power of this effect can poison everything and that's a road you don't want to travel down.

When you buy and save in multiples (literally)

I read somewhere that minimalism is likened to being an intelligent human, if you use it wisely. Speaking from personal experience, I cannot agree more on this statement. Having consciously practiced being simple in terms of my needs and expenses for some time now, I feel liberated every time I step into my house or my personal space. My life doesn't feel overloaded in the same way some of my colleagues describe their lives. The payoffs of being this way are incredible, and that's putting it mildly.

For instance, a while back, I mindfully switched to one bank account that comes with one card and a single PIN. Simple. Sure, I probably won't be making the best monetary gain every time, but I'll take it without any thoughts in exchange of the time I save and the peace of mind I gain. In essence, it's allowed me to function efficiently and happily and I'll settle for those feelings any day.

Break the habit — Take charge of your brain and actions

The key is to start small and start soon. Begin by asking yourself if what you have or what you want is something that you actually need. You can introspect and rely on your instincts or you can follow the Buddhist monk Ryunosuke Koike by putting your hand against your chest when you are unsure about an item. If you feel uncomfortable, then that's a sign that what you want is an indulgence and not something that you particularly need. The discomfort, he says, is a sign of your higher self telling you that you already have everything you need to be happy. You now have to believe it.

Let go of the idea of 'someday'

A lot of people live their lives through procrastination. They always think about 'someday' and forget to do what they have to do today. Some people collect empty tins and beautiful bags thinking they might come in handy someday. Others hold onto books that they've read several times with the thought that they might read it again someday. Some keep unused bags and old dresses that don't fit thinking... someday. That's what they tell themselves. However, that someday might never come.

Live in the present and look at what you have today

"The distinction between the past, present and future is only a stubbornly persistent illusion." — ***Albert Einstein***

Do you need everything you have? Is there something that you've saved for someday? If you have things that you think you don't need and won't regret letting go of later, then I recommend that you let go of it today.

Points to remember

- Maintain alignment between what you feel you need and what you actually need.
- Resist the urge to believe you always need more.

- Recognize any signs that imply you are getting used to or getting dependent on things.
- Make value-based choices while taking into account intuition, research, and the bigger picture.
- Resist the urge to acquire in multiples.
- Resist the urge to think 'someday'.

CHALLENGE TIME

- Discard something right now.

CHAPTER 3 — GETTING RID OF THINGS THAT DON'T BRING YOU JOY

"Happiness is not having what you want, but wanting what you have." — ***Rabbi Hyman Schachtel***

At times, the urge to show off gets the better of us

It was a day like any other at work. During lunch, five of us found a corner table in the spacious food court and sat down to eat our meals.

Karen was the first to point out, "You look gorgeous, Cheryl. I love what you're wearing. It's fabulous."

"Make that we," Rachel jumped in.

"And me," I said.

Even with little or no make-up on, Cheryl always looked beautiful. She'd recently cropped her brunette crown into a bob and was wearing more make-up. Her eyes were blue like the color of the sea and she'd accentuated them with a champagne tone eye shadow. She'd completed the look with mascara and curled lashes.

Even her sense of fashion had changed. Everything in fact had changed — the dresses, the sweaters, the pants, and the shoes. All of it appeared color coded and well put out. Everything looked rich and felt in sync. She looked very beautiful, almost as if she had just stepped off the pages of a magazine.

"And that bag, where did you get it? It must have cost a fortune. I love bags and would love to add a piece like that in my collection," cooed Phoebe.

"Well, thank you guys," Cheryl said. "I wanted to try a new look and so changed my wardrobe. I'm glad you like it."

"Like it, we love it," Rachel went on. "I mean, where did you get all these? They're amazing."

"Yes, tell us. I've devoured catalogs and made so many trips to malls, but everything is too pricy and nothing comes as good as these," Karen agreed.

"Well, maybe you need to look closer. I got most of my stuff from the mall right opposite our workplace. And guess what, they're still on sale," Cheryl beamed, knowing fully well that she'd hooked us on a date for some retail therapy.

Now, I don't particularly remember wanting anything, but I went anyway.

The mall was decked with advertisements, all describing the sale and how great it was. People flocked everywhere. There was the option of stopping to eat to re-energize on the topmost floor too, with just the right kind of finger food to nibble on while we shopped.

"This place smells like happiness," Rachel screeched with delight.

Phoebe was completely taken in by all the stores, her eyes widened, her pupils dilated with anticipation and excitement.

"This is happiness," the others unanimously agreed.

Phoebe got the branded bag she wanted. Plus some branded shoes and clothes to match.

Karen joined in with some designer dresses, a pair of ankle-length leather boots, and a pair of Gucci sunglasses. Rachel got herself a new haircut at the same place that Cheryl had got hers, and while at it, she decided to get herself a fancy manicure and facial as well. I myself don't remember actually buying anything, but I was happy to tag along anyway.

The world of conspicuous consumption[1]

By definition, conspicuous consumption refers to a lavish or wasteful spending mindset to display economic power, enhance social status, and to flaunt one's riches. This doesn't necessarily refer to all expenses because sometimes you do get your money's worth and end up spending much less in the long run. It refers to expenses that are solely for the reason of show, where some people tell the world that they have newer stuff and fancier experiences than others through their purchases.

When who we are with and what they own becomes the foundation of what we own and become

In one way or another, most people are victims of conspicuous consumption at some point in their lives. People can often be judgmental and like to share their assumptions with others. So in a way, what others perceive of you and put out into the world about you is what you come to be known as. Irrespective of whether you are convinced or not, the people holding the microphone should be convinced, and that's really where the problems start to occur. The process of image-building is so subtle but deep, so evident and normal, that some people can feel almost obligated to endorse it. They therefore become a creature of habit and feel obligated to buy things just to convey their 'qualities' to others. The more they collect, the harder they need to work to build the image they've advertised through it and their collections begin to grow.

Their purpose then shifts to increasing their brand value and with it their belongings. They, therefore, spend an enormous amount of money and time chasing that image and maintaining all that they've accumulated in pursuit of it. When you equate material things to personal qualities, you start believing what you own is what you are and then end up living your life maintaining and managing your so-called 'new identity', and we all know that's a road that has no end.

Self-worth (or the lack of it) lies at the base of nearly all our actions

Human beings are social animals. Most people are designed to love and feel happy when a person loves them back. They feel dejected, upset, angry, and depressed when the person they love loves someone else or cheats on them. Often, they seek meaning not from inside of themselves but from recognition and acknowledgment of others. They are unable to see value unless it is projected from another's perspective. In their bid to find value, they try to fit in and adhere to society's so-called 'accepted norms', and in the process become victims of conspicuous consumption.

We pursue perfectionism as the means to approval, acceptance, and love

How often have you shared something about yourself in anticipation of the validation you know you'll get from it? Most people feel happy when someone likes something they share. They feel even better if they feel appreciated and receive praise because of this, and even more so if they share their achievements with others. It's the number one reason why most of us are on social media platforms. Most people want instant recognition and they want it in multiples of thousands. Clearly, they find their worth from their recognition.

Some individuals who are rich want people to know they're rich, and so their worth comes from having a chauffeur open the car door for them or displaying art masterpieces that cost a fortune. It makes them feel valued. Some want to feel included and fear missing out or being left out and so they subscribe to the existing model of conspicuous consumption, even if they inherently don't endorse it. Others use accessories to proclaim their importance. They want to tell the world they are worth it but can't scream that out because that just isn't 'cool', so instead, they wear expensive sunglasses and jewelry, and branded clothing.

Being the social animals that humans are, most people can't bear to live without thinking they have value. Sadly, for most people, value doesn't come from what they are but from what they own. The truth is exactly the opposite. Value comes from digging deep inside. It comes from knowing you are worthy by birth. And it comes from giving, sharing, and caring for others and not the other way around.

Conspicuous anti-consumption: Getting rid of everything that isn't you

A major part of doing this comes from introspection. Only when you live with yourself, alone with all of your thoughts and chatter, will you be able to embrace, address, and see everything that isn't you for what they are. You'll be able to distinguish your inner-calling from the background noise. Once you begin to understand who you are and what you want from life, you'll be able to surround yourself with thoughts, people, and things that bring you joy. That's also when you'll know what you don't want and will be able to make efforts to get rid of them.

Get rid of things that are in multiples

It's easy to let go of things you have in multiples. Some people are guilty of holding onto multiples and, over a course of time, lose track of how many of the same items they have. As a result, their space becomes cluttered and, amidst it all, things get lost. Go through your belongings and evaluate everything that you own in multiples. I'm not talking about the necessities but the things that you don't use and, therefore, don't need. Try and reduce them to only the things that you use. If you already don't stockpile unnecessarily, then you're on the right track. Good job.

Get rid of things that don't bring you joy

The first step to getting rid of any unwanted things is to recognize everything that you own. Most people buy out of impulse and don't really have a purpose to it. As a result, they end up hoarding things. Go through your belongings and make a list of 20 things you have, then go through them again, but this time deliberate on what each of those things means to you. If they bring joy to your life, then they have a purpose and can stay. If they don't, then it's time you say goodbye to them.

Abandon the notion that you can't discard your things

We are trained to think that we shouldn't let go of things that have a certain materialistic value to it. In other words, you want to get rid of things but fight the urge because you feel you might be going against the rules of not valuing things enough. However, there are no rules. You are free. So how do you plan to exercise that freedom?

The key is to break the habit. It is to only buy things that you need and know you will use within a reasonable timespan. If you stop buying unnecessary things for the future, you'll have fewer things to discard. That said, if you already have things that you've bought and know you'll surely use them in the near future, then by all means hold onto them and make sure you use them when the time is right. But if these things aren't something that you're going to use, then discard them right away.

Points to remember

- Self-worth lies at the base of all actions. You are not the sum total of what you own.
- Perfection comes from being the best you can be, not from being what others want you to be.
- Get rid of everything that isn't you.
- Get rid of things that don't bring you joy.

- If who you were wasn't what you wanted to be, then it's time to say goodbye to who you used to be.

CHALLENGE TIME

- Become aware of your last conspicuous consumption. Why did you do it?

CHAPTER 4 — THE PSYCHOLOGY OF ATTRACTION THROUGH SIMPLICITY

"One day I will find the right words, and they will be simple."
— Jack Kerouac, The Dharma Bums[2]

The Japanese were minimalists

Back in the day, a traditional Japanese individual owned no more than four kimonos because that's all he needed. He kept fresh and clean. He lived light, needing half a tatami mat to sit and one tatami mat (about sixteen square feet) to sleep. He ate lightly, but sufficiently. He kept active and his legs were strong enough to take him from one place to another. Homes too were kept intentionally simple. People were nomadic by nature and keeping the structure of their homes simply meant they could be easily rebuilt.

Perhaps it exists in Japanese culture?

This simplicity is evident even today in one of their most revered ceremonies in Japan. Traditional tea ceremonies, called Sado in Japanese, is a time to socialize and celebrate. The ceremony includes a ritual of preparing and serving Japanese green tea, called Matcha (which is a little bitter in taste) together with Japanese sweets, so as to symbolically balance the bitter and sweet experiences of life.

Conducting this ceremony with the right spirit is extremely important in Japanese culture. The room consists of a tiny door that also serves as the entrance. The Japanese believe that only those who nurture feelings of concord, respect, purity, and calmness can walk through the door, and so by virtue of entrance, you are worthy.

Even samurai warriors were asked to leave their swords behind before entering the room. Here, it doesn't matter if you are poor or rich, warrior or peasant, VIP or not, everyone is equal and are treated as equal (with respect, kindness, love, and importance). Everyone is present solely to savor the taste of a cup of tea while making purposeful conversation.

Shintoism and Buddhism[3], the two major religions in Japanese culture, propagate minimalism as a way of living in simplicity. Much like minimalism, these religions endorse the idea of introspection and making your own choices, and of living them too. The Four Noble Truths in Buddhism explain how desires and ignorance lie at the root of all suffering. It explains how fixing a desire with material things gives birth to momentary and false gratification and how, by virtue of its temporality, that spirals our quest for more and more.

The beauty of both teachings is how they induct you into the system of simplicity and minimalism without ever trying to rush you into it. A major part of the wisdoms is directed towards self-realization, meaning the lessons are personal and relevant to you. It teaches you to be mindful of your thoughts and actions. When you are, you realize (within the time between thought and action) what you need and what you don't need, and what you should keep and what you should not.

Buddhism speaks about letting go of desires and emotional baggage in the most organic way possible — gradually and without any sense of aversion, guilt, or regret. But to do so you need to take time, give time, and become your real self when you are ready to be. The wisdoms transition you to be minimalists by nature, and by choice, thought, and deliberate action until you reach a point when you seamlessly just become.

Taking a leaf out of their book

Minimalism resembles and reflects the teachings of Buddhism and Shintoism in more ways than one. Because Buddhism and Shintoism induct you into the minimalist system in the most holistic way, it makes sense that we take a leaf out of their book. They're inspirational and teach things we can all learn and benefit from.

Getting real

The thing about minimalism is that it doesn't recommend working from a space of scarcity, meaning it doesn't ask you to get rid of everything you own simply because you need to have less. It asks you to reflect on buying endless items and instead buy only those that bring value to your life. The process of introspection before action and reaction encourages you to know, observe, recollect, distinguish, notice, and then determine whether you want something or not. It is rational, relevant, and replicable and so you're more likely to stay on course and transform for good.

Extending your new self to your relationships (especially romantic relationships)

When you work on yourself and become your most authentic self, you'll no longer feel the need to fit in or pretend. On the contrary, you'll find it very difficult to say and do things that you don't mean. While this might affect your relationships at first, over a course of time, people might (and I say might simply because it involves matters of the heart and therefore cannot be generalized) begin to love your simplicity and authenticity. You might begin to attract people who resonate with your current understanding and this can do wonders to your dating and love life. With minimalism and authenticity by your side, you might even find your soul mate. Again, this is by no means a rule of thumb. The point I'm trying to make here is that when you are your most authentic self, you're likely to become less conflicted, and therefore might attract like-minded experiences into your life.

Understand the opposite sex before you attract them

Speaking from a female perspective, I have noticed that many men don't notice the fancy stuff women spend all their money and time on, let alone care for it. Most of what women do — and I'm talking about the likes of over-the-top hairstyles, nails, and make-up — are things we do to ourselves for want of compliments, acknowledgment, and love. What makes it worse is that we do them on the pretext of believing it is what is expected of us and that it is the norm. Some of us believe men expect us to look a certain way so as to be attractive. We, therefore, blindly follow the norm at the cost of looking like exact replicas of each other.

The reality might be completely different. For instance, I once asked a male friend of mine what their idea of a good date and a good conversation was. I wanted to know what was at the very top of his list. He mentioned that, at their core, the majority of men are no different from the majority of women. They want to know you and the thoughts that run inside your mind. They want to understand your belief systems and find out if it resonates with theirs. They want to know if you are the right person for them, if they can spend the rest of their time with you, if you can contribute to their personal development by guiding them when necessary. They want to share their ideas and know if they resonate with you. They want to know if you can imagine sharing your life with them. They want to listen to women too and that's why, like women, they also value conversation and compatibility over everything else. To think all men have the same thoughts as my friend's would be silly, but his answers may provide some insight for some readers.

You are attractive, **not** because of your facial features, but because of what is reflected in your soul

If you believe your identity comes from the layers of façade you carry with or on you, then it's time you give yourself a reality check. Don't let the totality of your being be defined by the things that you put on in order to keep up appearances. These things contribute no value to your existence and do little or nothing to your evolution. Instead, accept and love your most natural self. By that I mean channel your inner beliefs through your physical appearance. Let your inner beauty talk. Likewise, let your choices and sense of style reflect your belief system. Because when you do, when you take away or minimize the importance of these frivolous and external things, you strip the inconsequential. You focus on things that are purposeful and add value to your life by developing your personality, intelligence, social skills, and emotional intelligence. You become your most authentic self, and that is by far, the most beautiful thing to be.

Your vibe will attract your tribe

The beauty of your soul is the most irresistible thing. It is the basis of true and lasting attraction. Just as you discard the unnecessary from your life, you will become a beacon of light in an otherwise crowded and cloned world. You won't need an app to help you find a date. All you have to do is make an effort to put yourself in situations where you can meet people, and people will have no choice but to notice you. They will want to get to know you and be in your company. You will attract respect, love, and companionship through your sheer presence.

Practice being attractive without falsehood

A relationship with any future, particularly with your partner, has to be genuine. It has to be based on mutual attraction, desire, and respect. Be real and keep things as they are because you want to attract someone who understands your priorities and mindset towards life. You want someone who understands that you won't be spending time on unnecessary things or giving them fake compliments. Because only when you are devoid of any falsehood and are your authentic loving-self, will others love you for what you are. They will love you knowing that despite any hardships, you'll always be genuine and do your best for them. Authenticity always wins.

Follow your intuition: Now that you know your true self, trust it

While dating is instant and mindful, connecting with your partner or soul mate might happen at a subconscious and almost spiritual level. Those who've found life partners or soul mates always find it difficult to express, in words, how it really happened simply because it happened beyond the levels of reason and judgment. So stop reasoning and listen to your inner voice. It knows better.

Here's wishing you a happy, loving, and enriching romantic life

Whether you want to date and keep it casual or step into the dating arena in search of love and companionship for life, having a romantic life that makes life that much more fun and meaningful is something most of us want. And everyone can have it. Some just don't realize it. If you can be true to your conscious and put out the real you, you'll most certainly attract like-minded relationships into your life. Remember that when you are your most authentic self, you are also your most attractive self, and that's when magic happens. Happy times are just up ahead.

It worked for me — it will work for you too

I'll let you in on a little secret. Believe it or not, while I believe there's absolutely nothing wrong with doing so, I've never used a dating site or app. My minimalistic choices have allowed me to work on myself as a whole. It has helped me think differently — not out of force, but by choice where I say and do things I connect with and endorse. It has helped me look at the world in a whole new way and I find that intrigues and excites people, more so the opposite sex. I always found myself wanted and ended up attracting potential mates everywhere I went. It's not because I am prettier, a flirt (I suck at flirting — trust me), or that I would physically try to draw attention to myself, but because I am different. I come across as real because I mostly do and say things that I genuinely mean and that makes people think I'm different (or so I'm told by my friends). I speak my thoughts no matter how weird, nerdy, or politically incorrect they may seem, and I guess that's what makes me unique. By simply eliminating the extras and being my most authentic self, I've created an aura that makes me interesting and mysterious, respected and important, unique and attractive according to some.

Points to remember

- Extend your real self to your relationships.
- Let your inner beauty talk. Focus on things that are purposeful and add value to your life by developing your personality, intelligence, social skills, and emotional intelligence.
- Your vibe attracts your tribe. So stay authentic.

CHALLENGE TIME

- Ask a friend(s) to name a few of your authentic traits.

PART 2 — MIND

CHAPTER 5 — THE PSYCHOLOGY OF CLINGING ONTO THINGS

*"You only lose what you cling to." — **The Buddha***

It's been a long day at work and you've spent most of it staring at a screen, toggling between emails and folders of information. You notice a pile of files stacked on your desk just as you are about to leave, but decide you'll attend to it the next day. The way back home isn't any different — there's noise from traffic and the wait time is the same. You walk past your door and are met with piles of newspapers and magazines that you don't have time to read. There' a pile of plates and cutlery lying on the counter and you decide you'll clean them all once you've finished dinner. There are dresses thrown on the bed, and an empty glass and some wrappers on the table. Oh wait, there's some laundry that you need to fold too.

It's all. Too. Much. And you wonder, "Is it just me?"

You are not alone

Sadly, feeling suffocated and unsettled by and in your own home is not as rare a situation as one might think. According to a research by UCLA's[4] Center on Everyday Lives of Families (CELF), the amount of stress you carry with you is the end result of the number of unnecessary things (and I mean physical and emotional) you amass.

The purpose of the study was to determine the influence of clutter on the lives of people. Researchers carefully studied the lives and behavioral patterns of several middle-class, dual-income families with kids.

The results[5], although alarming, weren't surprising, and are detailed in a book produced by the team entitled Life at home in the Twenty-First Century[6]. Families that lived amidst clutter:

- Were less happy and more irritable.
- Had unhealthy patterns of the stress hormone cortisol.
- Felt inadequate and ineffective.
- Felt shameful and helpless.
- Had difficulty in meeting their commitments and daily chores.
- Lacked a work-life balance.
- Were more inclined to get depressed.
- Were more tired and frustrated.

So why then do people buy so much stuff? And why can't they get rid of what they don't need?

There are a multitude of reasons for this, some of which are detailed below:

- ignorance and/or denial of the situation
- unaware of an alternative
- uncontrolled emotional impulses (we have plenty of advertisements that feed this)
- memories of the past
- fear or anticipation of a future need
- guilt
- obligation
- out of sight, out of mind
- scared of 'wasting' things
- sentimentality
- don't know where to begin

Science can help provide a more definitive explanation

Allow me to introduce you to a genius at play — the human mind. The human body is constantly changing, regenerating billions of different functions simultaneously to develop into a more efficient self. What's more, the driving force behind these miraculous accomplishments is the tiny little sponge-like substance sitting in the upper region of your head, called the human brain. In essence, your brain is orchestrating a symphony of complex functions within your head every second, literally as we speak. Undoubtedly regarded as the most powerful organ in your body, your brain is responsible for your thoughts, moods, reflexes, emotions, speech, and habits. In essence, it's that which defines you and makes you do all that you do.

Your brain consists of more than a billion neurons to act out the functions you perform. In order to do so flawlessly, they converse with each other by emitting electrochemical signals back and forth through neural pathways[7] and synaptic connections[8]. These neural pathways, which evolve throughout your lifetime, facilitate your neurons[9] to communicate from different activity-specific regions inside your brain. Every time your brain performs a similar activity, the neural pathway involved to perform it becomes stronger. This explains why habituated routines are easier to perform, whereas a routine that you are trying to learn is not so easy.

Your brain is conditioned to act out your habits — All it needs is a known stimulus

Have you ever noticed how certain stimuli[10] in your surroundings make you act in certain, almost predictable, ways? As though you don't realize what you're doing but you do it anyway? You just can't help it.

When you repeat certain habits in similar surroundings time and time again you become conditioned to respond to those stimuli, irrespective of whether you want to go through the activity or not. This is the reason why reforming alcoholics are told to stay away from bars. The conditioning process that they've set up over years of practicing unfavorable habits is now dominant enough to make changing or overriding them feel almost impossible.

Difficult yes, but not impossible

If you want to overcome destructive habits, you have to find ways to create life-changing neural pathways that override the existing unfavorable ones you've seeded and matured over years of practice. Now that you know how your brain works in acting out habits and how you've single-handedly trained it to be the way it is, you should know that its transformation is also in your control. Instead of thinking that something is wrong with you or that you will always be stuck with a nagging habit, think of what you can do to undo the habit. Think of how you can re-write the negative neural pathways with positive ones.

They all add up

We live in a society that's quick to judge and brand. What's worse is that they are equally quick to sell their assumptions to others. It's good dinner-time conversation, you see. You either fit in and get included or rebel and get ignored and nobody wants that. Most people need attention and acceptance and need others to make them feel worthy.

Society is the product of our inbred need to be with others of our own species. In essence, it reinforces our need to be with others like ourselves. We are exposed to ads that tell us what we need to be healthy, good looking, successful, and happy. We are given formulas that promise to fix just about anything instantly. As we seek to satisfy our need for acceptance and while in pursuit of things that society tells us we need (and the number of these things only grows), some people become hoarders by habit.

Justifying lack of control by giving it sentimental value

In essence, our possessions can symbolize our hopes and dreams. They can represent the world that we want to fit into. They can personify what we want others to think of us as. However misguided it might be, looking at these things can bring back memories and reinstate the reasons you bought them, and fill a void that came from a lack of security, status, comfort, love, and worth. With that much sentiment riding on these things, it comes as no surprise that it can be difficult to let them go.

They tell our story

People hold onto things because they attach them with memories and/or hope, says June Saruwatari, author of *Behind the Clutter*[11], a thought-provoking book that entails not just the physical things that occupy our space but also the mental clutter that keeps us from living in the present and being happy. She explains how we buy things in the hope of accomplishing something that's been left undone for a long time. As long as the thing stays, our hope to complete the undone remains, and due to that hope of fulfilling the task someday and fear of missing out, we refuse to let it go.

We hope to lose weight and therefore buy a treadmill. We hope to catch up on reading and therefore borrow fifteen of the most loved books from the library. We hope… and therefore we… Somehow that's always the narrative. We validate our excuses by attaching it to hope and that one feeling alone is enough to keep you going.

We hold onto things because we fear not valuing it otherwise

Some people refuse to let go because of the monetary value they attach to something. For instance, you've bought something that was highly priced and know you'll lose out on money if you resell it or give it away. You therefore hold onto it so as to justify the monetary loss you might have to suffer otherwise. Sometimes, because the item isn't really worth anything any longer, you're faced with the option of keeping it (although it is not worth anything) versus cutting your losses. Other times, the thought of losing out on money and of not valuing things might trigger memories from the past, such as a time when you might not have had enough. You, therefore, hold onto things because you believe you've learned from your experiences and don't want to go down that path again.

It's a vicious cycle borne out of fear, and that manifests into a compulsive and self-destructive habit

The need to experience the feelings mentioned above can cause us to cling onto more and more, in time compounding into the reactive burden of living amidst all the memories and physical baggage associated with these things.

Until you realize you have had enough and want to reform. Because you can...

Ask yourself why you can't part with your things. Let's face it; there might only be a handful of people who are ready to drop their possessions overnight and they may not be the ones reading this book. Decluttering is a positive response that is acquired over deliberate introspection and action. Fortunately, you don't have to rush into things. Take your time and, when you are ready, focus on each item you have trouble parting with and ask yourself why. Dig deep and stay open. You might be surprised by the not so obvious answers.

Memorabilia are different from memories

So often, we hold onto physical belongings because they help us recollect a certain memory. You hold onto your first paycheck because it reminds you of a certain time. You hold onto your baby's first car seat because it reminds you of the day you got him/her home...

However, there isn't any relationship between our past and the records we hold onto in view of recollecting that past. You are quite capable of remembering any memory from the past, and if you happen to forget a certain memory, it probably was something that was okay to forget. It's okay to move on.

In essence, it's the memories that we can recall without the aid of physical possessions that are important. The rest amounts to frills and extra possessions. As for photos, I recommend you go digital. You'll be saving up on space and can still look at them when you want.

Let go of the idea of getting your money's worth

Nobody likes to lose out on hard-earned money, and so in view of getting our money's worth, we hold onto things even when they become irrelevant to our situations. For instance, you hold onto the bike that you hardly ride and let it collect dust because you aren't getting your money's worth. Well, the truth is that you most likely won't, but it's okay to drop your expectations just a bit. Get real and make the sale when you think you've got a good enough deal.

Minimizing is difficult, but not impossible

I believe that cluttering is not just the physical manifestation of your impulses. It digs deeper and into emotions that are stopping you from realizing yourself. Decluttering the physical things can actually help you unravel layers of unaddressed and suppressed emotions. When that happens, you'll realize your true self and will begin to live your best life.

Points to remember

- Clutter causes stress and anxiety. Stop subscribing to it.
- Your brain is conditioned to act out your habits- so cultivate the right routines.
- Memorabilia is not the same as memories. Take pictures, but it's better to go digital.
- Let go of the idea of getting your money's worth.

CHALLENGE TIME

- Name three things you possess that you have been conditioned to hold on to. Now let go of two of those items.

CHAPTER 6 — THE TECHNOLOGY DIET

"Let it go. Change the channel. Turn it off. Unsubscribe. Unfriend. Unfollow. Mute. Block. Walk away. Breathe."
— ***The Minimalists***

Technology has forever changed the world we live in

It isn't often that one gets to experience a life-altering revolution. This is exactly what happened to the previous generation who were mesmerized by the innovations of the computer and speak of their first experiences with enthusiasm. However, those of us who have grown up with devices can't quite appreciate this. Instead, we're transfixed by what's easily taking the world by storm and constantly changing.

The likes of social media and social networking alone have changed the internet, almost in the same way the internet has changed us. With platforms such as Instagram, and Twitter firmly establishing themselves as social media sites, each one of us has the power to take center stage and present our ideas to the world at any time we wish to do so.

For the very first time, people now have the opportunity to showcase their skills to a broad audience from the comfort of their preferred spaces — something that was previously reserved for major television networks and wealthy advertisers. Whether you want to share your life and mood, promote your business, broadcast an idea, or start something new, your window to connecting to the world has become bigger with social media.

The question is whether all that showcasing and sharing is good for you

My answer is NO. I love technology and absolutely love all the great things you can do with it. It helps manifests dreams, create jobs, and connect with people. But it can also infiltrate into our lives if we don't know how to handle it. It can consume our time, and with it consume our energies to work on other important tasks. In essence, it can take over your life and that's something I am not willing to let happen to me. Fortunately, I've learned to use technology more mindfully and use it as a cheat for handling my daily routines. Sadly, that's not the case for everyone.

Life has quite literally become focused on eating, sleeping, and consuming via social media

"Scrolling is the new smoking." — ***Joshua Fields Millburn***

Technology has changed the way we function as social beings. As Sean Parker, co-founder of Napster, rightly puts it, "It has changed the very meaning of being social[12]." Now, experiences trump over material goods. The conspicuous consumption of goods that defined your status, wealth, and power has made way for the conspicuous consumption of pictures and videos that tell people where you are, what you did, and whom you were with.

The world needs to know about you and you are ready to let them in

How you feel, what you do, and what you have done is regarded as prized social currency — the more you share, the more your currency grows and the more valuable you become.

Fame comes in an instant

Because technology allows you to capture and share every mood so beautifully and because so many are on social network sites — more than a billion are on Facebook, and more than 100 million use Instagram each month — recognition is instant and so is validation.

And you become obsessed

All this matters because status matters. If you have high status, people laugh at your jokes more, you earn more, and you get invited to more parties. You are more liked and your image of being loving is also believed.

Narcissism

In an interview[13], Sam Vaknin[14], author of the book *Malignant Self Love: Narcissism Revisited*, compares the ill-effects of social media to that of epidemics such as Ebola and AIDS. He says the viruses that cause these epidemics are self-limiting in the sense that they restrict their effect so as to propagate and thrive. If the virus affected everyone, everyone would die, including the virus. Therefore, in order to survive, the virus attacks only some people. This way, it is guaranteed a continuous supply of host bodies. He believes social media has the same effect on people, only it's more discrete and sinister.

He adds that social media has a deep impact on the psychology of people. He states, "People aren't only competing with others and the markets they do business in, but are also competing with themselves. If they gathered 2000 likes for a post that they uploaded yesterday, then they've already set a benchmark below which they cannot score." This, he believes, can put undue and extreme stress on an individual.

Speaking from a clinical psychology point of view, Mr. Vaknin confirms what studies on social media have revealed; that expressing positive feelings require a lot more words than expressing negative feelings. Sentences such as "I love you" and "you are doing great" are never enough, making the receiver question why the giver couldn't convey more. On the contrary, single words such as ugly and fat are more than enough to cause detrimental effects on the same individual.

Mr. Vaknin says some social media platforms are actually built to make most of us need more. He quotes the former chief engineer of Facebook who, while communicating regret for his actions, revealed that they built the platform for addiction and with negative features. He believes that because of the way social media is built, people are sometimes forced to interact on a superficial level. They can never reveal their real side because if they do, they risk revealing a side of them that is vulnerable and 'not society-approved' in the process, and thus can expect to be virtually stabbed to death. He believes social media has exponentially multiplied the number of negative interactions, and with it, the amount of pain and stress an individual on such platforms goes through. He concludes that all of this has increasingly made some people narcissistic, when what they're actually trying to do is protect themselves from being hurt again.

People want repeated validation from others

Value is at the center of our existence. Most people feel valued and happy when others like, share, and subscribe to their views and end up fostering an addiction through a dopamine feedback system[15].

If it's good, then they'll tell us so. If you're good, then they'll tell us so.

Today, it's come to a point where some people are unable to go through life without wanting continuous external stimuli in the form of recognition and acknowledgment from others. And that's big — giving that much power to others over ourselves can literally break people as instantly as it can lift them up.

Trolls, threats, things going too far, and not thinking ahead

Social media[16] is hurting our mental health at large. One of the main reasons people become depressed or consider suicide stems from their lack of value. Sadly, technology is very quick to ship the letter that says, "DO IT, DO IT NOW!"

Trolls and malicious comments by people who don't know enough or have nothing better to do are given way too much relevance, even overwriting rationale and truth sometimes. It's their word over ours and so they always win. So many youngsters (some even in their teens) are being affected by this dangerous phenomenon. Surely this needs to stop.

We need to change

Sadly, most people live their lives backwards. They pursue happiness, not on the basis of what it means to them, but on the basis of what it means to others. They see others lead a certain life; become convinced that this is the 'good life' they want to live and go about chasing things that can eventually get them there.

Well, it won't, simply because they are running in the wrong direction. Happiness comes from within. It comes from a space of knowing you are precious by virtue of your existence. It comes from knowing you have enough and from valuing everything you have. It comes from being and not showing. When you are all these things, you most likely will become your happiest and most attractive self. Likewise, you'll most likely find everything and everyone around you equally attractive. You won't need others or technology to tell you that. Just yourself.

"Our tools are only as good (or bad) as the person using them."
— The Minimalists

Drop your antenna

The amount of information available today continues to grow at an explosive rate, and sometimes consuming too much information can lead to a state of stress, anxiety, insomnia, and depression. Minimize the time you spend on TV and technology. Minimize the exposure to the news too, thus completely eliminating any irrelevant and negative news that might subconsciously affect your state of mind. Instead, only watch stuff that brings value to your life and helps you evolve for the better. Surround yourself with positivity and positive people. Think of ways to improve your knowledge. Sharpen your skills and think about ways you can use those newly acquired skills. The world surely needs doers like you. How can you make it a better place?

Cut social media out of your life or minimize it

Social media is not one of the most fundamental technologies of this century. It absolutely is not. It is a source of entertainment[17]. Period. After all, we've not needed social media for thousands of years. We did fine without it. Now people think they're not happening enough or their lives are over if they are not on it. Given how it endorses an environment in which people become obsessed with attention, can't think and act on their own, and feed off other people's failures, I believe it's something we can definitely do without, or at least do with less of.

Dorothy, 23, says quitting social media has helped her identify her real friends. "I'm more productive and less concerned with what other people think about me now," she says. "Now, the only person I compare myself with is me and I work hard to be a little better than yesterday."

If deleting your accounts all at once is a little too hard-hitting for you, then inch your way towards it. Start by minimizing your time on it. Only use it when you have to, and only for positive reasons. Cut the urge to comment, share, and like. There are a million opinions floating around already. One less won't do anyone any harm but will do you a world of good.

Extend the technology diet to your children

For those born post-2000, technology has been an integral tool in their lives and education. For those born post-2010 and those that will be born in the future, technology is life. Moreover, the line between virtual reality and actual reality will be thinner. So how do you instill technological minimalist values in your children when all their 5th-grade peers have smartphones? Reason with your children, educate and reward them for their time spent away from their phones. Prematurely introducing the addictive dopamine feedback system mentioned above can only have detrimental effects on impressionable growing brains. It is difficult to predict how your children will react to the technology diet, but although it may be difficult, it is definitely worth a try.

Minimize TV time

TV is always the backup in homes. We're so used to the one-in-one-out approach that when we minimize social media, we most often spend that time on TV, which is equally bad. Cut your cable connection if you have to or only watch shows that are of high caliber and that you are passionate about. Remember, you don't have to go on a binge and don't have to watch every other show just because your friends are doing so. Don't settle for mediocrity. You're destined for much more. Spend your time reading positive and educational information. Likewise, minimize your exposure to negative news, and instead spend that time honing a skill. How about spending time with your loved ones, or spending time doing the things you love? Learn to paint, play an instrument, or write that book you have always wanted to write.

I speak from personal experience

Over the years of working with technology and getting drawn into its world, I've realized how easy it is to get lost with it. I've seen friends lose their personal life to it, seen them regret it later and struggle to fix things. Now, I must admit that there have been times when I felt the urge to give in too — to dive in a little deeper and spend more time on it, but I quickly learned to mend things.

For instance, I found a lot of my friends used apps on their phones to help achieve their tasks. I tried it too and, to be honest, it did help me at first. However, I soon realized that the mere routine of setting reminders meant I had more reasons to be with my phone, and somehow they always extended to more screen time with it. There's a certain amount of technology fetishism that creeps in. I quickly learned to not try to solve common life problems with apps and software programs. Some things should be kept basic. If you don't have discipline, an app won't help.

Another time I developed a habit of checking emails every morning and night on my phone from the comfort of my pillow. I felt stressed and annoyed because I couldn't help responding to some emails. My work time stretched to my rest time and I wasn't happy about it. Now I try not to keep my phone on my nightstand. Instead, I charge it in another room and only pick it up when I am ready to work.

I've benefited in so many ways

I love technology because it helps me grow and evolve, learn and explore, dream and become. But I don't consume it to the point that I get consumed by it. I ensure I mindfully keep my time to only what is needed. I also keep my time on TV to the bare minimum and am not personally on any social media platforms. I cannot emphasize how happy and liberated I feel as a result of this.

I value relationships and spend my time nurturing them. I value time and, therefore, spend it wisely. I also value myself and protect myself from being scrutinized, judged, ridiculed, mocked, and bullied as a result of that. I also protect myself from needing to be praised, of having my ego massaged, 'liked', and 'shared'. I simply don't want to be someone's frivolous dinnertime conversation (no one really wants to be either) and so focus my energies on being the best version of myself. There's plenty to do because it's always a work in progress.

Most importantly, it has given me more time, and I cannot emphasize enough how much this has catapulted my growth!

Time, they say, is a gift worthy of the Gods. It is what allows you to flower into that irresistible person. Cutting back on technology has given me time to nurture myself and my relationships. It has helped me create new opportunities for my personal and professional lives. I am able to work on things that genuinely interest and entertain me. Sure, I might have not seen the meme everyone is talking about, or found out what happened to a certain reality star, but then, what good does knowing that do for me anyway?

Points to remember

- Our tools are only as good (or bad) as the person using them. Use technology for what it was built. Use it constructively and sparingly.
- Social media can be sinister. Avoid it or minimize your time on it.
- Social media is not one of the most fundamental technologies of this century. It absolutely is not. It is a source of entertainment. Period.

CHALLENGE TIME

- Delete selfies. How about we start by keeping one for every ten of them?
- Delete email subscriptions (and I'm talking about the ones from online clothing stores, emails given at the checkout/cashier in stores etc.). You don't need another reason to buy and hoard.
- Don't go on any of your social media platforms this weekend. Take stock of the experience on Monday. How did you feel? Could you possibly be addicted to social media? What did you spend your extra time on?

CHAPTER 7 — DEVELOPING HEALTHY MIND-STIMULATING ROUTINES

"If you hear a voice within you say you cannot paint, then by all means paint and that voice will be silenced."
— ***Vincent Van Gogh***

Simple words, but with a wealth of wisdom and so very liberating to say the least.

As much as I might come across as mostly sorted, there have been times when I have felt a little less sure, and there will be more times like this ahead because that's the way we are all wired up. We go through moments (however brief they might be) when our mind coaxes us into doing something we don't want to do or into not doing something that it believes we can't do. I'm no different and have had my moments of inner conflict — not because I didn't know who I was and what I wanted, but because I felt different and thought I had to fit in.

I felt conflicted soon after graduation because I was being pulled in every direction to meet this person or that group and go to every party I was invited to. I didn't want to because I didn't see the value in many of those outings, and with being involved in the drama between this person and that person, and the gossip that went beyond reality as well as the judgment that came with it. To me, this was (and still is) useless information that wouldn't bring any value into my life.

I'd receive texts from friends describing an alleged break-up/make-up between couples when I didn't care for the information. In fact, I've always found this kind of information intrusive. I'm troubled by how some people can, without thought, dig up stuff from other people's lives and concoct them in such a way so as to make them gossip-worthy news.

My mind said, "Don't encourage it," at times, and, "But what if they feel bad," at other times. I was conflicted and felt bogged down by thoughts of losing out on friends and hurting someone unintentionally. I also always thought I wanted to fit in. My personal life began to suffer, and with it, my peace of mind too. Soon it started creeping its way into my work life. That's when I realized I had to do something to address the situation I was getting myself into. It was during that phase that I was able to find a way to rise above my doubts and fears and truly accept my individuality.

Now, the process of getting there was not without mixed feelings. A part of you, your mind, holds you captive, replaying events that tell you to do otherwise. These doubts and fears are yours and feel very real. They feel legit and can convince you to do what they want you to do. But these feelings are nothing but your mind's way of dictating terms. Because, when left to it, your mind will want to run your life for you.

Fortunately, I was quick to realize this and began creating checkpoints to address and eliminate such unfruitful thoughts. Then I began courteously eliminating relationships and conversations that didn't resonate with my ideologies for life. As I continued to do this, I did my best to address the inner chatter inside my mind.

I dug deep and questioned everything that I felt wasn't me. The deeper I dug, the more I discovered and the more authentic I became. As a result, I had more control over my mind. I was able to build a core group of solid real friends who talked about things of value to me and we as a group were able to help each other lead a more meaningful life. I continue to go back to that framework every time I feel conflicted or bogged down by my thoughts. The fruits paid off and here I am writing this chapter for you.

Distorted thoughts

In essence, an untrained mind is terribly wavered and has a tendency to constantly drift between periods of the past, present, and future. An amateur mind has no place to call home and wanders restlessly, in search of inner peace and happiness. Its need to settle down the restlessness forces it to shuttle between various thought patterns, each thought trying to brush aside the uneasiness caused by the other.

Think about it. How often do you find yourself drifting towards mindless inner chatter while at work? Let's look at the past hour for instance — how often has your mind wandered to thoughts outside of this book? Well, if you're like most people, then I'm guessing the answer is, "Quite often." Just as you stay seated reading this book, your mind is probably thinking of ways to distract you. Suddenly, you find your mind worrying about unfinished tasks at work. You might even find it lingering around last night's dinner conversation, debating on who said what and why?

You see, even as you will yourself to stay focused and rooted to the present, your restless mind will have a plan of its own, making it difficult for you to concentrate and center your thoughts.

The thing about clutter

Clutter is the breeding ground for a terribly wavered mind. As emotional beings, people tend to associate their belongings with emotion. In many ways, they perceive their possessions as being a part of their identity, an extension of themselves, so to speak.

What you own can tell your story

For instance, if your clutter consists of other people's stuff, then you might have problems with setting boundaries. Likewise, if your clutter is mostly memorabilia from the past, then you might have a tendency to hold onto stuff, people, and their memories. Maybe you're not ready to let go of the relationship or your memory of it and that's stopping you from letting go of the clutter? This can make the process of letting go very painful for many people.

Psychological effects of clutter on our minds

In fact, there's scientific proof[18] to indicate that there are undesirable feelings associated with being walled in by clutter and positive feelings achieved when decluttering.

Clutter can:

- Increase the levels of the stress hormone 'cortisol' in your brain.
- Induce feelings of shame or inadequacy that can lead to depression.
- Distract you from focusing on things that bring productivity.
- Negatively affect your mood, and with it your relationships with your loved ones.

Dr. Rick Hanson, author of *Hardwiring Happiness* and speaker at a *TED Talk*[19], describes how cortisol can result in actual structural changes to our brain, causing long-term sensitivity to stress:

"Cortisol gradually stimulates the alarm bell of the brain; the amygdala, so it rings more loudly and more quickly. And cortisol weakens. It actually kills neurons in the hippocampus, which besides doing visual-spatial memory, calms down the amygdala and calms down stress altogether," he says. "*The mind can change the brain which can change the mind,*" he continues.

All this can gradually change the structure of the brain (especially if stress is chronic) and can ultimately lead to us feeling worn out and low. This, in turn, encourages us to buy more comfort items or cling tighter to the ones we currently have. It's a vicious cycle that needs to be broken.

So how do we break this chain?

Revisit your childhood

As the professional organizer Regina Leeds[53] says, "In order to begin the change process, examine where you come from." She believes that the roots of people's inability to organize stem from their formative years, through the modeling and messaging system they get from people who've influenced them (parents, teachers, siblings, relatives, and friends). Sometimes, the inability to declutter might come from a nostalgic experience. "These decisions often go beyond a cognitive process and include a deeply emotional one," she goes on to say.

In order to fix the outside space, we must turn inward. Understanding the reasons for our clutter can help find ways to overcome them. We must, therefore, clear our head before we clean out any physical clutter.

The key is to shift to a state of mindfulness

Mindfulness, quite simply, is the ability to live in the moment and observe your mind from an outsider's perspective, without any sort of judgment, bias, or criticism. When you are mindful of your thoughts and inner feelings, you create an additional 'cognitive layer' of yourself, one that consciously observes and records everything you do, only with the same intensity and emotional disconnect that you'd exhibit while observing an outsider. By being mindful, you'll be able to enjoy life's experiences that much more!

Do one thing at a time

While it might be mentally challenging and satisfying to multi-task, in reality it can become the very reason you have a drifting mind. If you find that your mind is quite wandering to begin with, then it's important you train it to stay rooted to the present for longer periods. Start by single-tasking. Go through your tasks one at a time. Resist the temptation to knock off a few tasks all at once, however easy the task might seem. As the Zen proverb declares, "When walking, walk. When eating, eat." Only then will you be able to train your mind to be in the present!

Do not rush — Do everything that you do slowly and deliberately

While going through your tasks one at a time will surely help you stay in the present, rushing through them won't. In addition to single-tasking, it's important you take your time and move slowly. Try and stay as aware as you can. Go through your actions with deliberation and purpose and you'll soon find it easier to center your restless mind.

Do less

Call it the domino effect. By having less, you will have fewer things to keep in order and more time on your hands to do tasks mindfully. If you do things one thing at a time and as deliberately as you can, then you're likely to take more time to get through your tasks without distractions and will hence be able to do less than you did before. While I'm not asking that you stay negligent and shirk away from your responsibilities, I ask that you choose wisely. If you can consciously prioritize tasks, you'll be able to figure out what's important and what's not.

Space out tasks

So often, we breeze through things without thought or focus, only to realize that we've lived that moment without being fully aware of it. Give your tasks the time and respect they need. Do not crowd your mind with one task after the other. Instead, leave room between things that are on your schedule. Utilize these 'spaces' to re-align your thoughts while bringing clarity and purpose to it.

Journal your dreams

Recording your dreams, especially memorable dreams from the past, can be a good way of addressing any pent-up feelings. Record your dreams on a daily basis. Read it to yourself and reflect on it. Track it too. Do you see a pattern? Do you always dream of particular themes? Write them as you remember it.

As you begin to read your journals, you'll realize new things about yourself through your own experiences. In time, your journal will become a unique personal treasure of sorts, a priceless home of insight to work through your traumas. They can help you find solutions to some of your most haunted and long-drawn concerns.

Practice meditation and breathing and spend a few minutes every day doing nothing

Yes, I said nothing!

Some of us seem to be stuck with the idea of setting our mind to chase after something; goals, thoughts, dreams included. But it's equally important that you drop all your mental wandering and see yourself as you really are every once in a while. Simply sitting in silence and focusing on your thoughts and breathing will teach you ways to overcome your mind's resistance to living in the present.

As you progress further into these practices, you will become more aware of your thoughts and will be able to brush aside the relevant from the irrelevant ones. When you enter this zone of mindfulness and living, you will notice your breath integrate seamlessly with your mind and body. You'll also notice your mind stay willingly inside your body, recognize a sense of peace flow through it, and finally feel your entire being reverberate with a sense of higher consciousness and superior productivity!

When you've completed the practices and feel happy within yourself, take a few moments to surrender to the powerful energy that vibrates within you while staying grateful for the liberating experience.

Points to remember

- An untrained mind is terribly wavering. Meditate in order to bring it to the present.
- Similarly, clutter is the breeding ground for a terribly wavering mind, so mindfully practice decluttering.
- Clutter causes stress and poor mental health. Start by letting go of one thing at a time.

- Understand the reasons for your clutter. Revisit your childhood memories.
- Shift to a state of mindfulness. Mediate and practice mindful breathing.

CHALLENGE TIME

- Meditate once a day, three times this week. Or, if you're a beginner, go outside into nature and stare mindlessly at a lake, animals, a tree, etc. Get lost in it. Take stock of the days you meditated and the days that you didn't. What differed between the days?

PART 3 — BODY

CHAPTER 8 — MINIMIZING YOUR CLOTHES

"It is always the simple that produces the marvelous."
— Amelia Barr

In a quiet and residential area in North America, a slim, tanned, flawlessly dressed young woman called Katie walked into her walk-in closet.

Her hair had been colored blonde and her natural roots were beginning to show. She was almost ready — her skin flawless and dewy, her lashes thick and curled, and her hair tied into a sleek bun.

"But I can't find anything appropriate," she muttered to herself, her eyes widening in disbelief. "I have a ton of clothes, but absolutely nothing to wear."

Katie had a lunch date with her boyfriend in 30 minutes, but here she was, still in her house staring at her closet and wondering what to wear, believing she lacked choices.

Her wardrobe might have told a different story to others. Her apartment was truly tiny, but the closet inside was huge and jam-packed. Clothes lay stacked neatly, one on top of the other. One could shop here — pants were on one side, shirts and t-shirts on the other. Dresses hung neatly on individual hangers. The top shelf was occupied by seven or eight bags, each of a different color, size, and look. She had a little more than a dozen pairs of shoes too, all neatly stacked in a closet right next to the front door. She really put a lot of thought and effort into her wardrobe and should have felt she had everything she needs. But she didn't. She always felt shortchanged and spent a large part of her weekends buying make-up, clothes, and accessories.

"I don't have anything appropriate. These aren't trendy enough," she muttered before half-heartedly choosing a dress for the afternoon.

Turns out that Katie is not alone

The average American spends more than $1,100 on fashion each year, buying as much as fifty new pieces. Now, before you begin tracking and justifying your last purchases (which I am sure you already are), let's stop for a moment to really ask the big questions.

What is it about fashion, clothes in particular, that makes it so attractive to you? Why can't you just wear the same thing every day? Why does style play such an important role in your life? What exactly do style and fashion mean to you? And while we're at the topic, why, when you spend so much and have so much, do you always feel a sense of loss?

Take a moment, several in fact. This will take time and is probably something you need to keep asking yourself time and again.

Your wardrobe has a voice

Fashion can be different things for different people. It's fun and channels a creative outlet. It's a chance to experiment with colors, shapes, textures, and understand what they mean to you. It's also a way of finding and expressing yourself. Your clothes reflect your choices — they reflect your personality and what's important to you.

They tell a story

The dress you wore on your first date, the oversized sweater you love to curl up in, your wedding dress, your mom's wedding dress which is now yours, the denim shorts that you wore on your summer vacation a few years back — they all have stories and are a snapshot of memories from your life.

If I paid for it and if it's in my wardrobe, then I'm keeping it

Because we are very loss-averse and fear the possibility of losing out, we struggle/refuse to let go off things that aren't relevant anymore. But that's exactly where the delusion lies: the money is already spent, the memories will always remain, and so there is nothing left to waste except for your time, energy, and closet space.

Fashion is a form of art and expression, but it should also be functional

You want your clothes to look good on you, but you also want them to make you feel good. A functional wardrobe is one that fits into your personality and lifestyle. Consider the stuff you do, places you go to, and the people you meet. Does your wardrobe support you in your present environment? Is it relevant?

Letting go

Here's an activity you can do every three months. Go through your apparel and let go of anything that doesn't fit you or reflect your personal style, is way too uncomfortable, and/or makes you unhappy in any way.

"The value of a man should be seen in what he gives and not in what he is able to receive." — ***Albert Einstein***

Figure out the stuff that isn't working out

Remember, just because something isn't relevant to you, it doesn't mean someone else won't love it! Find a new owner for it and move on.

Donate or sell

If a piece is still in good condition, then it should be valued and given to someone who can use it better. Donate your pieces to a charity shop or give them to a friend who may like them or put them up on sale.

Keepsakes

If you must hold onto sentimental pieces, restrict them to only what's most meaningful to you and store them safely in boxes. Think of it as a sort of trial separation. If, after a period of time, you have a change of mind and think you are ready to part with them then do so. And if not, then rest assured, they're safe in the box.

Finding a balance

The key to maintaining a functional and fashionable wardrobe is simple:

1. Keep key pieces that truly reflect your personality and sense of fashion.
2. Keep pieces that double up and can be worn in lots of different ways.
3. Keep statement pieces that add variety to your looks and help you express different facets of your style.
4. Stock versatile monochrome basics that balance out bolder pieces and give you something to fall back on any time. Pieces that come in black, white, brown, olive, khaki, and pastels are never out of fashion and go with almost everything.

Be open to change: Building a minimalistic and functional wardrobe will always be a work in progress

Even the most meticulously curated closet isn't meant to be forever. Your style is ever-evolving, just like you are.

My relationship with my wardrobe

Over the recent years, I've consciously made an effort to be more mindful of the things I buy and accumulate. I understand my body better now and have discovered fashion styles that suit my body type and reflect my personality. I've learned that more is never enough and having what you need and being content with it is the best way forward.

This thought has seamlessly echoed in every aspect of my life, and that includes in my wardrobe too. To my mind, clothes should be treated as a secondary extension of oneself and nothing more. You wear the clothes, but the clothes don't wear you. Likewise, you as a person need to override that judgment with who you are. Your wardrobe is your tool to express yourself. Use it to empower you and not enslave you.

Your go-to person should be YOU

The people I admire the most for their style aren't those that follow every trend. These people are mostly real people with real lives. They don't dress in designer wear from head to toe, but they've always caught my admiration (and many others) with their sense of style. They are style icons not because they follow rules but because they make their own. They are strong individuals with strong characters and that reflects through in their thoughts, actions, conversation, clothes, and way of lifestyle.

The perfect wardrobe isn't something that you can concoct in a weekend

Because most people base their purchasing decisions on quantity rather than quality and on trends rather than personal choices, they never take the time to figure out how they want to dress and what type of clothes would actually work for them. They buy clothes on impulse and end up with a mishmash of things that neither suits their style nor their lives. So despite having a large and full closet, they feel a sense of lacking and end up buying more and more of the same stuff.

This is how hoarding begins — It's time you recognize it

Your wardrobe becomes a band-aid, so to speak, to stick on your ever-diminishing sense of authenticity. Your sense of identity becomes tied with your appearance. Everything becomes a quick fix and we all know that they don't last. I believe there's no point in buying five crappy shirts for cheap only to have you itch and stop wearing them the next month. Instead, invest that money in something you know feels comfortable and will last for years. Longevity and quality are paramount. Less is more.

Keeping it simple, light, and just right

My friend Sushi has taught me a lot about fashion and style. She loves fashion just as she loves dressing up and looking good. But she dresses to feel good and she says she only feels happy when she is herself. She says she, therefore, avoids buying things that don't reflect her personality and doesn't spend her money on seasonal must-haves. She says years of experience have taught her to buy less than before but choose better. She says she might own fewer clothes, but always has something nice to wear and I couldn't agree with her more. Having known her for years, I've always admired her sense of style. I've also noticed that most of what she owns doubles up as other pieces and that gives her wardrobe a very unique twist. That is, you might have seen some items but they're not always worn in the same way as before. This is what makes it refreshing and attractive to people, including to me. I've learned from people like Sushi and try and incorporate their tips into my choice of wardrobe. Speaking from personal experience, I can't tell you how liberating it makes me feel.

It has made me happy and I want the same for you!

Drawing inspiration from people like Sushi, I now channel my wardrobe as a form of expression. I've learned that what's inside is more important than what is outside, and I don't need 100 pairs of jeans, 200 shirts and 50 purses to express that. Over the years of learning from others as well as my own experiences, I've developed a strong sense of style. I've also become my own best stylist and have built a great wardrobe that works for me. It makes me happy and I'm very grateful to all those incredible people who've helped me get to where I am.

Speaking from personal experience, I believe this mindset can help a lot of people. Sadly, many people live their lives conflicted like Katie. They can't stop feeling they need more, and therefore continue to accumulate without ever putting the things they acquire to full use. I understand just how depleting this journey can be. After all, no one wants to be conflicted. If you're currently in the mindset of Katie but want to break the habit and consume less, then I want you to know that I'm here to help you.

Points to remember

- Be authentic. Create your own unique look.
- Fashion is a form of art and expression. But it should also be functional.
- Be selective. Reserve your closet space for items you love 100%.
- Aim for quality over quantity.
- Let go of any extras every three months.

CHALLENGE TIME

- Throw out (or give away) everyday clothes you haven't worn in the past three months (keeping any seasonal essentials you need).
- Color coordinate your wardrobe. This will save you time and help you style your outfits.

CHAPTER 9 — BEING BEAUTIFUL

"You're the only one who's worried about your face."
— Ichiro Kishimi, Fumitake Koga, and Kirawareru Yuki (Courage to be Disliked)

As I thought about what I wanted to share in this chapter, walking around my garden while sipping on my favorite tulsi-ginger[20] tea, I was pleasantly surprised by the reflection that stared in front of me.

The person in front of me had a sparkle in her eyes that mirrored the clarity and sense of peace she felt from within. She had no lines of worry, and in its place, had clear and supple skin that felt loved and nourished. Her body looked fit and strong, like it had earned every toned muscle it showcased. Her hair was naturally voluminous and had a shine that bounced off the reflection. Everything about her looked so in tune, as if her body was an extension of her state of mind. This woman looked happy and very, very much at peace.

I credit this rather bold judgment to feeling as positive and happy as the reflection in front of me. I believe it comes from a space of acceptance and belonging from the one person that matters: me.

If you're anything like me and spend only what you need to on beauty products and services, but instead choose to spend your money on traveling and introspection, then you'll know what I'm talking about. Being someone who believes that beauty comes from within, that your most natural self is also your beautiful self, I cherish what I have and nourish it with plenty of love, positivity, and some basic things that I will share with you in this chapter.

Simplify beauty

Here's the thing I've discovered with beauty and pretty much everything else in my life: the more product or external 'things' we use, the more dependent we become to them. Dependency can soon become necessity and obsession, so here's my solution below.

Let's start with the skin

Your skin is your largest organ. It is also the first place to show any signs of dehydration, stress, and aging. It makes sense then to take care of it and give it the attention it deserves.

Take it all off

Natural Wash

The foundation of a great skin care routine starts with a clean, bare face. Get rid of any make-up and let your skin breathe. Coconut oil[21], apple cider vinegar[22], a mix of honey and lemon[23], and fresh grape pulp[24] (red or green) work like magic on the skin. Simply dab/massage one of these onto your clean skin. Then throw a warm towel onto your face to open up your pores. Wait for 20 seconds and pat dry with a clean washcloth.

Regular Wash

Everyone's skin is different. So, make sure to pick a pH balancing cleanser that works for you. The fewer the chemicals the better. Massage the cleanser on your wet face for over 50 seconds. This allows your pores to be thoroughly cleaned out.

Tone

Next up is toning. It helps your skin re-balance its natural pH levels after cleansing while prepping it to absorb what's to come next — moisturizing. Rosewater, aloe vera, witch hazel, and willow bark[25] are great natural choices.

Moisturize

Proper nourishment is the key to healthy and glowing skin. Fortunately, regular moisturizing does that. Again, stick to nature. Olive oil, coconut oil, almond oil, shea butter, castor oil, argan oil, and aloe vera extract are great on skin. Identify your skin type and pick a mix that's most suitable for you.

In addition to the above tips, here are my best beauty routines. They are simple, but effective. I urge you to start with the basics and build from there.

Apple Cider Vinegar (ACV)

Applying ACV can do wonders to treat acne-prone skin. With an alkaline property that balances the pH levels of your skin, it proactively kills acne-causing bacteria and absorbs any excess oil on your skin. Additionally, you can also use ACV for healthy nails.

Honey and Cinnamon[26]

The antimicrobial property of cinnamon and the anti-bacterial property of honey can help you achieve that healthy, clean, and youthful skin you're after.

Milk and Turmeric[27]

Drink a glass of warm milk mixed with a teaspoon of turmeric every day. The anti-inflammatory and antioxidant properties of turmeric work well with milk to fight acne and other skin blemishes.

Yogurt, Turmeric, Fullers Earth, Gram Flour, and Honey[28]

Fuller's earth removes dirt. It also unclogs pores, prevents whiteheads and blackheads, fights acne, and reduces lines and wrinkles. Apply a mask made from a mix of yogurt, turmeric, Fullers earth, gram flour, and honey. Rinse off after letting it rest on your skin for 15-20 minutes.

Moving on to your hair

While your face is usually the first thing people notice about you, your hair is what frames your face. It's therefore important that you give it some thought and love too, in the most natural way, of course.

The Basics

Here are some of my favorite health care routines. I keep going back to these miracle mixes every now and then and cannot stress strongly enough what a world of good it has done to my hair.

Oiling Your Hair

Try a warm mix of coconut, almond, olive, and castor oils. They restore damaged scalps and nourish hair with essential vitamins. You can also dab a little of this mixture on your nails. The saturated fats from the oils do wonders to replenish weak and brittle nails.

Avocado

Blitzed avocado, honey, and eggs[29] can do wonders for your hair and scalp.

Rosewater

Rosewater has incredible beauty benefits, both for skin and hair. Make a mask by mixing two eggs, a cup of rosewater, and four teaspoons of almond oil[30]. Apply this mixture onto your scalp and rinse after 20 minutes.

Lemon Juice and Coconut Milk[31]

Most often than not, it's your dry hair that's causing all that frizz. Nourishing it with natural conditioners such as lemon juice and coconut milk will leave you with surprisingly straighter locks and defined curls.

Coconut and Castor Oil[32]

This remedy really works for hair growth and is my go-to before every wash. Mix and heat a tablespoon (each) of coconut and castor oil. Let it rest for a few minutes. Once warm, massage the tonic onto your scalp and hair, rinsing it with cold water after an hour of resting.

Eggs and Olive Oil[33]

Mix a few drops of olive oil with two whole beaten eggs. Massage the mixture onto your scalp and hair to strengthen and condition your hair. Rinse it with cold water after an hour of resting.

Vinegar[34]

Vinegar is an excellent conditioner. For this remedy simply dilute a cup of vinegar with three cups of cold water. Rinse your hair with the mixture right after washing your hair.

Rice Flour, Eggs, and Fuller's Earth

Create a mud mask by mixing five tablespoons of rice flour with a cup of Fuller's earth and an egg. Apply the mask on your hair, making sure you comb it through to the ends. Let the mixture work its magic for an hour. Then, once dry (it might be crispy or flaky too), rinse your hair with cold water. Rest assured, you'll be taken in by the incredible results.

Aloe Vera Gel

To moisturize dry hair, mix fresh aloe vera gel with a cup of warm coconut oil. Apply the mask on your hair, making sure you comb it through to the ends. Let the mixture rest for an hour, rinsing your hair with cold water after an hour of resting. You are welcome!

Got Curls? Try Ayurvedic Treatments

Create a hair mask like those detailed above, but add Henna[35] powder for damage repair (only on darker hair), Amla[36] fruit/powder for accelerated growth, and Shikakai[37] powder for defined curls and strength.

Simplify further

Hold onto three or four hairstyles that you love and believe looks good on you. For instance, for people with long hair, you can do a top knot, a man bun, a pony, and/or leave your hair loose. You can accessorize these styles to give them variety. Likewise, men and women with short hair can use accessories to give them a different look. Mixing it up can be loads of fun so don't stop experimenting.

Cutting/Trimming Your Own Hair

Before you panic, I want to assure that it's actually easier than you think. Look on YouTube for some ideas and quick fixes if you need them. There are plenty of techniques that are as easy as securing your hair in a ponytail and then chopping it. Additionally, invest in a good quality hair trimmer/clipper for shorter-length hair.

Create Curls Naturally

This one is mostly for the ladies. Wash your hair in the evening and sleep with your hair crunched into a bun or braided. Allow this to work overnight and wake up to waves/curls (depending on your natural hair type) that are unique and just right. This look works so well with everything, and it's natural, heatless, and very replicable.

Points to remember

- Simplify beauty. Discover beauty products and hairstyles that are easy and elegant. Discover what works for you.
- Avoid or minimize the use of make-up and styling products.
- Use healthy and natural remedies such as the ones mentioned in this chapter to accentuate your beauty.

CHALLENGE TIME

- Throw out make-up, beauty utensils, and products you haven't used in the past two months. Clean out your drawers and if there is something you know you'll never use, get rid of it.
- Ladies, I challenge you to go make-up free for seven days. It will do wonders for your skin.

CHAPTER 10 — WORKING OUT EFFICIENTLY

"Each new day is an opportunity to improve yourself. Take it and make the most of it." — **Gymquotes.co**

"Back in the day, when I first ventured into exercising regularly, I had no idea of what I was doing," says Martin, my gym instructor and a good friend of mine. "I didn't know what particular exercises were suitable for my body type and fitness needs. Neither did I know how many of each exercise I should be doing. I just did whatever came to mind, hoping and believing it would all work out in the end. I spent an hour or so at the gym every day and sat down at every machine for about the same time (somewhere between 15 and 20 minutes), before moving onto the next. I did this for a while before realizing that it wasn't working out. I got zero results," he says.

I connected immediately to Martin's words because, quite frankly, I've been there too. In fact, I assume a lot of people can relate to this.

"Fortunately, that was a long time ago and I've learned from then. I no longer have the inclination to waste time like that. My daily schedule is hectic and so if I'm going to put my time and effort into something, then I want the payoffs to be damn good. Over the years, I've learned that by consciously eliminating excesses, I can focus on what's most effective. I follow this in everything that I do and swear by the results," he continues.

I second his thoughts.

But in the world of fitness, there are a million options, choices, routines, and exercises, so how do you choose? Here are his answers.

You simplify

Sure, exercises can be complex, but there is a way to simplify your workouts. If you can build a minimalistic framework for fitness, you can focus on things that matter to you, on the essentials, and get rid of any frills attached to it. With this mindset, you won't need to invest in special workout gear (translating to more clutter). The basics will do and they are enough to keep you fit, healthy, and clutter-free.

Keep things simple and make them more replicable

Because time is a big factor in my life, I focus on putting in a minimum of 20 minutes every day and enjoy everything that I do in those 20 minutes. I am more mindful of those moments, of my breathing and my body's responses to the workout and, therefore, feel much better at the end of the routine. By keeping it short and simple, my brain has fewer reasons to procrastinate. I've also stuck to the routine for the longest time.

Bringing minimalism into the gym

Personally speaking, I place health and wellness over everything else. I exercise because I want to feel good, and to be and look my fittest. I therefore place quality over quantity. So you don't have to exercise for longer, but you certainly can exercise smarter. If you can approach your workouts through a combination of full-body workouts, high-intensity intervals, and compound movements, you'll experience satisfactory and sustainable results.

Compound vs. isolation exercises: My verdict

If you were to ask me to pick between compound and isolation exercises, then I'd choose compound exercises straight away, simply because they give me more out of my workout. Let me explain.

The movements involved in compound exercises[38] are functional and closer to our daily activities. That's because movements such as squats and deadlifts can be easily replicated in day-to-day activities such as sitting down or standing up. By working multiple joints and muscles at the same time, I spend more energy and, by that virtue, burn more calories.

Similarly, the multiple movements that take place during a compound exercise force your body to utilize more muscles to complete the workout. This in turn triggers a larger hormonal response of testosterone[39] which can then help repair muscle damage quickly so as to help you maintain your results. That's not all; compound exercises target multiple muscle groups or joints at a time, and save me plenty of time. And if you know anything about me by now, you'll know exactly why I am into it. Compound exercises kill (at least) two birds with one stone and I'm totally sold on the idea of more gains in this regard.

That said, isolation exercises[40] are by no means useless. They can help target specific muscles if that's what you want and can be a life saver if you're recovering from a specific injury. Curls, raises, and extensions are all typical isolation exercises. They work on specific muscles and work by doing just what their name suggests — they isolate.

By channeling all your attention on one muscle group only, these exercises can help achieve significant results in target areas. For instance, including a set of hamstring curls to target the hamstrings with a set of deadlifts can take your workout to the next level. They can burn and burn deep. By working on only those muscles, they put little or no stress on others (which is especially helpful if you're recovering from an injury). My verdict is to include a few isolation exercises that target the muscles you want to work on into your compound regime.

Here's my go-to workout plan (a mix of compound and isolation exercises) for the week. It usually takes me about 20 minutes to go through it, it's simple, easy to remember, and equally easy to track.

Monday — squats, assisted pull-ups, and wrist curls

Wednesday — deadlifts, flat bench presses, and dips

Friday — lunges, overhead presses, back extensions

The thing we call HIIT

High-intensity interval training[41] has been 'the-thing-to-do' ever since it hit the fitness scene several years ago. While its predecessor LISS or steady state involved cardio activities such as walking, cycling, jogging, and swimming, all done at a steady pace for a steady period of time, HIIT is typically done for a much shorter interval and involves manipulating rest periods so as to exert maximum intensity.

Now I love walking, running, and jogging, but I prefer to do it outdoors. It helps me connect with nature and is a great way to unwind and be with my thoughts. I have friends with similar interests and it's great to bond over a jog or a walk amidst nature. I love it and do it every once in a while when I have the time to indulge in luxuries such as this.

But on other days, I gravitate towards exercises that are effective and fast. HIIT, in my opinion, is designed for just that and fits into my life like a glove. It's super adaptable, meaning I literally can work out from anywhere, and is something I can breeze through very quickly without the guilt of losing out. HIIT helps me burn more calories at a faster rate. That's why I always include a few HIIT cardio exercises into my weekly routine. Here's what my HIIT workout for the week looks like.

Tuesdays — Walk and Sprint

Sounds simple I know, but I promise you, it burns and burns good. I do a 30-second walk, followed by a 30-second sprint and I repeat this seven times. Now, you can always do more, but by the time you get to sprint number four, you'll want to stop. Push through and do as many as you can without overexerting yourself too much.

Thursdays — Jog and Sprint

You're probably wondering whether there is a difference between this and the previous one. I assure you there is a big difference. This is taking it to the next level. So gear up! I follow the same pattern. I do a 30-second jog, followed by a 30-second sprint and I repeat this five times

Saturdays — Push and Squat

This too is simple to read but difficult to do. I do ten push-ups, followed by ten air squats. I then rest for 30 seconds and then repeat it. For more burn, alternate between one push-up and one squat until you do ten of each — that's if you can handle the intense burn you are going to feel.

Sunday — Sprint, Push, and Squat

Again, a combination of some of the previous ones because, as you know, I like to keep it simple. For this one, I start with a 15-second sprint, then drop down and do ten push-ups followed by ten squats. I rest for 30 seconds to one minute and then repeat the drill. This set hits most of my target areas and is relatively easy to remember. So you can channel all your focus on doing rather than remembering what to do next.

My fitness mantra

Having trained under Martin for over three years now, I can't recommend highly enough what is written in this chapter. I enjoy fitness as a means to stay healthy and active. I love traveling and enjoy the experiences being healthy allows me to have. I take good care of my body and it, in turn, helps me achieve the things I want to experience in life. The exercises discussed by Martin are the ones I keep going to every week. They suit my thought process and way of life — it is why they feature in my life. I like to keep things simple and I believe Martin helps me achieve just that. The exercises mentioned above are simple and easy, functional and effective. They save me a lot of time and I use that time to do things like sharing my experiences with you, so it's totally worth it.

Points to remember

- Exercises can be complex, but there is a way to simplify your workouts.
- Keeping things simple makes them more replicable. Focus on putting in a minimum of 20 minutes every day and enjoy everything that you do in those 20 minutes.

- Bring minimalism to the gym, and alternate between compound and isolation exercises.
- Practice HIIT.

CHALLENGE TIME

- Decide now that you're going to dedicate 20 minutes of your time every day to fitness. You can either reach out to the exercises listed above or find your own fitness routine. Journal your experience and create a milestone to chase every week.

CHAPTER 11 — CHOOSING HEALTHY FOOD OPTIONS

"Simple pleasures are the last healthy refuge in a complex world." — ***Oscar Wilde***

Being a university student in a different city really taught me a lesson on what we really need to survive. Limited funds meant you had to be creative. Thus began my journey into conscious and healthy eating. Every luxury I had at home, I didn't have access to at University. Therefore, I began focusing on healthy food options that would save me time and money.

For instance, I'd plan my grocery shopping ahead. I would plan what I would have available to eat for the week and make meals that lasted more than one day. After graduating and returning home, my minimalist habits had crystallized. Having predominantly been living on healthy food options, my diet is mostly made from plants and unprocessed foods. I eat plenty of vegetables and choose wholesome food ingredients over off-the-shelf ones, such as sun foods (foods that directly require the sun's energy) over junk and processed foods.

I gravitated towards a plant-based diet, intermittent fasting, and the ketogenic diet every once in a while. I've been this way for long enough to realize the long-lasting benefits from it. That is why, when I got back, I didn't want to change. I had transformed for the better and for good. I continue to follow this lifestyle and swear by its health benefits. Not only are these foods easier to digest, but they also stack high on energy. Simply put, I've never felt more alive.

Minimalism and your diet

Once you live by the idea that less is more, you might find yourself drawn to applying this philosophy to every aspect of your life, such as your diet and lifestyle.

Eating right and eating foods with healthier ingredients can improve your health and save you plenty of time and money. Here are some ways that I consciously try to simplify my food. I eat enough, I eat healthy, and I cannot be more satisfied with my food choices.

As always, start with the basics

The focus should not be on the quantity of food we consume each day — we only need so much food in a day, after all. What's important is that we get our daily dose of nutrients from it. Incorporating a daily diet plan that has the right balance of protein, fat, carbohydrates, vitamins, and minerals will keep you healthier, fitter, and more energetic. What's more, it will also do your skin and mood a world of good. Begin by thinking of food as fuel that acts as building blocks for your body to thrive. Once you shift your focus to nourishment, you'll be less inclined to consume food for taste or pleasure.

Reach out for plant-based foods

Nearly 25 gallons[42] of water is required to grow a single pound of wheat. Think of how all that water can be put to better use. Eat lower on the food chain and minimize the impact your diet has on the planet. Reach out for plant-based foods[43] such as vegetables, whole grains, nuts, seeds, legumes, and fruits. Also, decrease animal products if you can.

Keep it simple. Keep it real

Simple foods such as sun foods are great in terms of nutrition and taste. Likewise, choose healthy and minimalistic alternatives wherever possible. For instance, sprinkle olive oil and vinegar on your salad instead of loading it up with the usual mayonnaise and salad dressings. Simplify your life by prepping your meals in advance. Again, keep it simple. Having the right amount of protein, starch, vegetables, and fat can make up for a delicious and wholesome meal. You can also do light once in a while and opt for a huge serving of fresh salad vegetables topped with your favorite fruits and some healthy nuts.

Eat one thing at a time mindfully

When we speak about clutter, we mostly think of material possessions such as clothes, household items, cars, material possessions, and so on. Very rarely do we think of food as clutter, but if you look closely enough, there's plenty of clutter sitting on your plate at each meal and plenty more keeps going to waste. As part of being more mindful over the past few years, I focused my attention on food portions and what I serve on my plate. I now serve only what can be consumed at one time and serve more only when I need it. I also don't listen to music or watch something on the TV at mealtimes. When I'm eating, I'm only eating. I avoid any distractions, unless it is meaningful conversations that cannot wait for another time.

Eat everything on your plate

This is an extension of the previous point. When you clutter your plate with food, you take it for granted and don't really appreciate the taste, quality, or just that you're lucky enough to have food on your plate when some others don't. By serving what you can eat at a time, you can finish everything that you serve on your plate. As a result, you waste little of the food you make.

Stay hydrated

The key to staying hydrated is to drink nearly half your body weight every day, and this should be made up of mostly water. For variety, you can reach out to fresh green juices and some herbal blends which I will discuss in the following chapter.

Focus on quality

Minimalism in food isn't about simply downsizing portions of food. It's about simplifying your diet so as to make it easy for you and your body. It's about nutrition and quality over everything else. So prioritize right.

Food is not entertainment

These four words aren't mine to claim, but they've made a huge impact on the way I perceive and consume food. "Enjoy food more, but don't treat it as entertainment," says Jina, my nutritionist. She always reminds me of how extremely important food is to us. It is there to fuel and nourish our bodies. Having benefited so much from her diet and lifestyle tips, I agree with everything that she has said. Thanks to her guidance, I'm able to consume a wholesome diet that keeps me happy and healthy. I want the same for you and sincerely believe the tips mentioned in this chapter will help you achieve just that.

Points to remember

- Reach out for plant-based foods such as vegetables, whole grains, nuts, seeds, legumes, and fruits. Also, decrease animal products if you can.
- Simple foods such as sun foods are great in terms of nutrition and taste.
- Eat one thing at a time mindfully.
- Eat everything on your plate.
- Stay hydrated.
- Focus on quality.

CHALLENGE TIME

- Apply minimalism to your diet. Start with the basics. Declutter all the junk and processed food in your kitchen. Go on a fifteen day detox plan.
- If you aren't doing so already, begin preparing your meals with wholesome ingredients. Eat right, eat healthy, and stay hydrated. Evaluate yourself at the end of the month. How are you feeling?

CHAPTER 12 — HEALING AND STRESS RELIEF

"Healing yourself is connected with healing others."
— Yoko Ono

Most of the talk on minimalism is centered around the act of decluttering. But for someone who's embraced minimalism as a way of life, the real benefits come after the point of decluttering, when you have decluttered long enough to stop cluttering in the first place. It comes from the point of transformation — by letting go of everything that isn't necessary, you surround yourself with only that which you love and truly need. As a result, you experience some remarkable benefits for your mind, body, and soul.

Incorporating a minimalistic lifestyle can be a great way to detox and heal your body from all the wear and tear it goes through. In fact, one of the most obvious positive effects of minimalism is stress relief. When you live a minimalist life — and by that I mean you live in thought and action — when you let go of everything that doesn't give you joy and surround yourself with things that you need, when you declutter any negative possessions in your life and replace it with positive energy, when you stay away from toxicity and spread love instead, when you become all that, you'll be your most positive, loving, and healthiest best. In essence, minimalism is the simplest and most straightforward way of living healthy and happy.

Therefore, when it comes to the topic of stress and health, my stand is no different. I believe in getting to the root of things. I believe that fixing things through holistic and long-lasting choices is very much like decluttering your home.

When you dig deep and unearth the exact reason for your stress or illness, you'll be able to get rid of it. That's what I'm always after — If I'm going to spend my best effort and time on something, even if it is on myself, then the results should be worthy of it. I make healthy lifestyle changes that address the root of any problem as opposed to brushing it with make-belief and make-shift band-aids which are temporary fixes.

Healing the body and reducing stress the natural way

While I'm not a qualified doctor, I've spent enough time understanding my body to say this one thing: our bodies have the innate ability to heal themselves[44] if given the right conditions to do so. While healthy food acts as fuel for your body, sometimes fuel alone is not enough to replenish a damaged body. You might also need to give it rest, good sleep, and some very useful medicinal herbs. Here are some of the ways I take control of my health and give my body overall healing conditions to thrive.

Listen to your body — What does it say?

While this can sound different or unheard of to some, Dr. Deepak Chopra[45] believes it's the most natural thing to do. Your body knows better, and sometimes being intuitive will help you read the signs it's trying to convey to you. If you believe stress is your problem, try and understand what's causing it. Are you overloaded with thoughts, conflicts, and work? If you are, then apply the lessons of decluttering we discussed before. Go through your lists and rally on your wheel of purpose. Remember, what gives you joy stays and the rest — well, you know the drill.

Make some white space in your calendar

A great way to use minimalism for stress relief is to conserve your thoughts and actions. Practice the concept of thoughtlessness. Sometimes, thinking and doing nothing is the only thing you should be doing. Use the tips on how to say no if you must come up with excuses to buy some free time. Give yourself some rest and just be.

Create blueprints of what de-stressing looks like for you

We've discussed how your space can fill you up or drain you. We've also discussed how, through minimalism, you can create a space that revitalizes you. Use your newly-found minimalistic skills to counter any anxiety attack.

Top up with mood-boosting company and projects

Stress tends to unleash its ugly wrath at a time when you are at you're weakest. Keep yourself in good company. If this means working on your passion projects or spending time with your loved ones, then that is what you must do more. It prevents the stress from getting to you in the first place.

Get plenty of good sleep and rest

Looking around, I find people thrown into the torrent of multi-tasking. Everyone wants to be an overachiever and, in the name of 'increasing productivity', they have no distinction between work time and rest time. However, no matter how much you try to multi-task and over-perform, you'll never get everything done. So why beat yourself to a point where you lose your health and peace of mind over it?

I took a stand a long time ago; when I am in bed, I refuse to watch TV. I also charge my phone in another room. When I want to sleep, I stop thinking and simply rest.

Talking about sleep, here are some good sleep hacks:

- Go to bed an hour earlier than you ideally want to sleep.
- Adjust the temperature of your room. Keep it cool/warm, depending on your liking.
- Likewise, adjust the lighting in your room, preferably dark as light tends to disrupt sleep.
- Avoid heavy meals close to bedtime.
- Avoid alcohol and caffeine.
- Keep it quiet.

- Invest in a comfortable mattress.
- Do the same for pillows too.
- Try aromatherapy and warm salt baths.
- Listen to soothing music.
- Meditate.
- Surrender — sleep will happen.

I have written more about sleep in my previous book, *A Morning Routine*.

Consume adaptogenic[46] herbs and herbal teas

Minimizing or eliminating acidic beverages such as caffeine and processed and sugary drinks such as sodas and energy drinks can do wonders to reduce stress and increase good sleep. Likewise, consuming healthy liquids such as plain water as well as water with lemon, lime, or cucumber slices and/or mint leaves can keep you hydrated and energetic.

But if you want to give your body a quick reboot of sorts, then consuming herbal adaptogens, also called tonic herbs for good reason, might be the right thing to do. Herbal adaptogens are great because they help fight signs of chronic stress and its ill-effects on the body. They are great because they are safe, non-toxic, and have a calming influence on the body.

In addition to fighting stress and promoting good sleep, herbs can help you cope with stress, anxiety, and fatigue and also:

- balance sugar levels
- protect liver function
- get rid of toxins
- reduce sugar and alcohol cravings
- enhance immunity, energy, and endurance
- enhance stamina and mood
- help you recover from illness and injury more quickly

They come in capsules and herbal teas, are antioxidants, and hence eliminate free radicals. I've tried Rhodiola, Ashwagandha, Holy Basil, Schisandra, Ginseng, Cordyceps, and Licorice. I swear by their de-stressing and calming effects.

Points to remember

- Heal your body and reduce stress the natural way.
- Listen to your body. It knows better.
- De-stress with mood-boosting projects and company.
- Get plenty of good sleep and rest.
- Consume adaptogenic herbs and herbal teas.

CHALLENGE TIME

- Rummage through your pantry and get rid of anything that is processed, unhealthy, and addictive.
- Replace them with healthy beverages and herbal teas.
- Practice the points mentioned above and evaluate your body's health in a month's time.

PART 4 — SOUL

CHAPTER 13 — CREATING YOUR OWN SPIRITUAL PRACTICES

"When you realize there is nothing lacking, the whole world belongs to you." — ***Lao Tzu***

Throughout my life, I've been persistently driven and intrigued by questions such as: Who am I? What's my purpose? What do I want to do? And why do I act the way I do? Is it in tune with what I want to do? Is there a better way out? Why do I think differently from others? How can I be more authentic? How can I make the most out of my life? How can I stay happy while doing so? Is there a secret force that's behind all that guarantees happiness? And if there is, where and how can I access it? How can I use it to take control of my life and shape my destiny?

My obsession with experiencing a level of awareness and authenticity drew me inward. Over time, I began receiving answers, and I received questions too. I went back and forth with myself, bouncing off questions in search for a little more of me.

Over the years, I've learned and evolved through introspection. I'd like to believe I've come to a stage where I am more aware of who I am and what I want from life. I use introspection as an anchor to guide me on my journey to finding out increasingly more about myself, all the while being myself.

Through my experience, I've come to believe that every individual has the power to find themselves, and to virtually change anything and everything that exists in their lives so as to be their most authentic self. I've also come to believe that the resources we require to manifest these changes lie within us, waiting to be realized and applied all at once. In this chapter, I attempt to share my lessons with you.

The collective mirror: Leverage your strengths and limitations

If the only vision people have of themselves is the one presented to them by the opinions, perceptions, and standards set by society, their view of themselves will only be a distorted fraction of their true self. It is the view that society wants them to believe. However, it isn't entirely them.

Some people are so used to seeking acceptance from others that they rarely peek inside themselves for answers. Even their view of their strengths and limitations is predominantly based on the feedback they've received from others.

For example, others may say, "You're never on time." You may hear this and interpret it as punctuality definitely not being your strength.

"Why can't you ever keep things in order?" There you go again, not being as disciplined as you'd like to be.

"You must be an artist!" Meaning you're imaginative so a creative career is definitely on the cards.

"You eat like a horse!" You like food? No, wait, maybe you lack self-control?

"You always ace in math." So you'll work in finance or something to do with numbers! Definitely!

You see, a lot of what people believe are their strengths and limitations, and a lot of what you believe about yourself, comes from the sometimes distorted and out of proportion statements of others. These statements, if anything, are often more assumptions than projections.

This mirror that people keep going back to is largely determined by conditioning and environments set by society. While I acknowledge the incredible power of conditioning in our lives, to say that people are only that which they are made out to be by society is leaving a lot of our potential unnoticed. Amidst these uncharted lands lies our souls and it's calling. It's time you connect with it.

Projecting yourself outward: Accessing your inner-higher self

As you read this chapter, try to look at yourself from a distance. Take a step back and project yourself outward into a corner of your room. Now, look at yourself. What do you see? Can you look at yourself as though you're someone else? Reflect on your current mood. Can you observe it? How are you feeling? If you had to put it in words, how would you describe your current state of mind? As you peek inside yourself, try and focus on your mind. Observe how your mind is working. Would you call it swift and agile or slow and bored? Do you hear, at this very moment, your mind questioning the very purpose of this activity?

Your knack to observe and scrutinize yourself as if you were someone else is distinctively human. We call it self-awareness or mindfulness. It is your ability to separate from yourself and analyze your own thoughts and actions at will. No other creature, unless genetically altered, has this ability, which is why humans have dominion over all other beings in this world. It is also why they continue to improve and progress from one generation to the next.

This ability to reflect on our thoughts and actions as well as those of others is why we can observe, evaluate, judge, and imitate. We are not simply the sum total of our feelings, moods, thoughts, and actions. Self-awareness allows us to take a step back and understand our paradigms. It affects not only our attitude and behavior, but also what we recognize as our strengths and limitations. It acts as our map to building our character. The sooner we realize this the sooner we can get in touch with our soul and respond to its calling.

Meditation to connect with the essence of life and yourself

Many of us can perhaps agree that meditation is a life-changing practice in theory. However, actually putting it into practice can be a daunting task for some, simply because it's unknown and therefore complicated.

That's where most of us have got it wrong. Meditation isn't unknown or complicated; it's connecting with your most innate self. Also, it isn't any one particular thing you're connecting to — it's a state of mind.

People do different things to enter that state. There are several ways to get there, but you can choose to ditch it all and do whatever seems right for you. That's the beauty of it. You can use different methods as a point of reference, but I urge you to not complicate it with the opinions of others or hold it as a rule of thumb.

While projecting oneself outward is a great technique, STOP is another minimalistic meditation technique that I keep going back to. Try it and see if it makes sense to you. Likewise, improvise and make it yours.

STOP is a powerful meditation practice that helps me every time I need clarity. It's a simple acronym.

- **S**top what you are doing
- **T**ake a deep breath and pause
- **O**bserve your thoughts and responses
- **P**roceed to make the right choice or action

What meditation means to me

Meditation has transformed my life in ways that I cannot express in words (and that's saying something because I'm usually good with words). I try and fit in a meditation routine wherever I am, whenever I can, irrespective of the time. I meditate If I want to be with myself. I meditate if I want answers, have questions, am happy, restless, confused, and/or grateful. I meditate if I want to ditch bad habits, cultivate new ones, and/or slow down and in pace.

Meditation has helped me cultivate a deep understanding of myself and it can do the same for you too. Simply sit with yourself and observe. Keep doing that, and when the time is right, when you are ready, you'll teach yourself how to progress further, because in the end, it is your journey.

Points to remember

- Leverage your strengths and limitations. Get real and stay open.
- Make peace with your strengths and limitations. They are yours to embrace and mold.

CHALLENGE TIME

- Access your inner world by projecting yourself outward and getting an outsider's perspective of yourself. Do you like what you see? How would you like to be? What's stopping you from being that person? What can you do to get there? Start working at it.
- Meditate and reflect on your questions, their answers, and the silence and noise in between. Let everything flow without conflict.

CHAPTER 14 — CUTTING DOWN YOUR SOCIAL CIRCLE

"Have nothing in your house or your life that you do not know to be useful, or believe to be beautiful." — ***William Morris***

Part of my research for this book involved interacting with people and finding out about their experiences (which I'm sharing with you in this book). Some people spoke about how they used to accumulate before and don't do so now, why they changed, and how liberated they feel now. Others spoke about being simplistic from the beginning, but how despite being that way, it took them some time to realize it and accept themselves. They spoke about how they would try and fit in so as to feel like they belonged, but how it only made them feel more isolated. They spoke about how, only after gaining awareness about what they liked and what they wanted to invite into their lives, did they actually feel settled and included.

Gabrielle, a financial consultant and a friend I've made over the course of writing this book, has this to say about her journey: "There was a time in my life, about the time when I finished university and got my first big break, when I, for the briefest moment, tried to fit into, you know, society's definition of 'normal'. I'd made some friends while in university and they had friends of their own and we'd all hang out sometimes over food, coffee, and talk.

"Every interaction would play out to the same conversations — how wonderful one looked, how happy we were to meet the other, followed by the most happening gossip and event and why discussing it and being a part of it was what we were born to do.

"At first, I tolerated it a bit, mostly in a bid to fit in and not hurt my friends, but after a point, I couldn't stand the thought of attending another party or event let alone enjoy it. Funnily, as hard as I tried to be diplomatic and excuse myself in the most polite and subtle way, I got invited to more parties.

"Now, don't get me wrong," she continues. "It was very kind of my friends to want to include me in all their events, but somehow, I never fitted in. I simply couldn't get myself to poke my nose in other people's business, make up stories based on my assumptions, and ship it around to everyone I knew. As much as I liked these people, I didn't like what they did, and despite telling them several times, they never changed. For them, it was all harmless talk that helped pass time and made life interesting.

"This happened for the briefest bit after which I had to consciously keep a distance or decline repeated invites. Fortunately, I haven't had a change of mind since. Now, don't get me wrong again. I can keep friends. Some of the folks I am close to have been my friends for years, but they are also the ones I connect with and want to keep in touch with. We talk plenty, but only about things that matter and uplift us. As for the others, well, sometimes, it's better to part ways when you know it's not what you want," she concludes.

Well, I agree with Gabrielle and I can relate. I value friendship and will do anything to nurture a relationship if it is what everybody in the relationship wants. That said, if the people involved feel differently for a genuine reason and if a solution doesn't seem attainable, then I believe it's best to part ways on good terms.

"I'm as proud of what we don't do as I am of what we do." — **Steve Jobs**

Cutting down your social circle

When I decided to cut back on certain relationships and social circles years back, I knew very little about how that decision would unfold. I did so merely on instinct. I didn't feel like myself when I was part of conversations taking place within those relationships and that didn't make me feel good. I backed off because I didn't want to spend my time irrelevantly and irresponsibly, and boy, am I glad that I took that step. As a result of that one decision, I've become more mindful, productive, less cluttered, and happier. Plus, I've made friends who think like me and want things in life that are similar to mine. We share our thoughts and push each other to try harder and achieve more — it's a win-win relationship.

Science agrees

One study[47] found that people with fewer friends do better. It found that smart people experience lower life satisfaction when they socialize more. The findings also suggest (and it's no surprise) that those who are more aware of their potential are less likely to spend as much time socializing because they'd rather spend that time pursuing their goals.

And when you think about it, you'll realize it makes a lot of sense. When you know what you want and how to get there, you'll want to spend most of your time reaching for those goals. The super-intelligent don't like to waste endless time each day discussing irrelevant things with 'friends'. Instead, they are busy pursuing their goals, perhaps some that even involve changing the world.

People with a strong sense of self sometimes feel disconnected from their clan simply because they see the world differently. They, therefore, cut back on such company sooner or later and find like-minded people they can relate to. It's just a matter of time.

Learn to be okay with not being liked by everyone

If you continue to do things because you want to be liked and remembered by people, be warned that you're never really going to achieve it and might instead lose the opportunity to find yourself. It's impossible to please everyone, as hard as you might try to do so, so stop trying. Whether people like you or not is their business. Not yours.

It's okay to be alone

You don't have to follow people if it isn't something you want to do. It's OKAY to be alone. Ask me and I'll say it's great, because it's an opportunity to learn something new about yourself. As you step out to places you want to go and do things you want to do, you'll connect with people who think and act like you and that's a great place to start meaningful relationships.

Cut back on your exes if it isn't good for you

Some relationships are better off when not revisited. Relationships with exes can be one such thing. Romantic relationships are unlike any other relationship. We invest a lot of ourselves into them and, if in the unfortunate event that they end (especially if they end on a bitter note), a part of us caves in. It takes time to heal and move on, and so revisiting those people isn't always a great idea. Unless you're completely okay with them as acquaintances or friends and believe they bring the better out of you, stay away from exes, and spend that time on the present and on your future.

Stay away from toxic people

Toxic people are skilled at finding their way into people's life. Their game is practicable — they act very nice and befriend you, earn your trust, and then slowly manipulate and take over your life. They mean more harm to you than good and make you feel low about yourself. Cut out people you think are messing with your life. If someone makes you feel anxious, low, isolated, and alone, then they are not the right ones for you. Gain control over your circle of friends. End the relationship and protect yourself from negativity. You deserve better. Peace and happiness are around the corner.

Get out and try new things

You know what you know so far in your life, but pushing yourself to explore new arenas can help you tap into a part that you perhaps aren't familiar with yet. Alone time can promote self-awareness. You are always enough company for yourself.

So how are you going to spend your alone time?

Points to remember

- Cut down your social circle if they bring negativity into your life.
- Don't waste endless time each day discussing irrelevant things. Instead, use your time constructively and on purposeful projects.
- Likewise, spend your time with people who resonate with your thoughts and can help uplift you.
- Learn to be okay with not being liked by everyone. If it isn't working for you and it's causing you harm, then it's okay to back out. Stop trying to please when you know it'll harm you.

CHALLENGE TIME

- Delete those contacts you haven't talked to in over a year from your phone. Instead, get out and try new things. Gain new experiences. Document them. How do you feel?

CHAPTER 15 — SETTING HEALTHY SOCIAL BOUNDARIES

"I encourage people to remember that "No" is a complete sentence." — ***Gavin de Becker***

I've reached a new boundary-setting landmark — I had an entire weekend of nothing but reflection, creating, and sharing.

I spent the entirety of Saturday and all of Sunday just thinking about everything that I wanted to share and put together in this chapter. No window shopping with friends, no texting and no phone calls, no dining out, and no watching a movie either. Absolutely nothing. I haven't stepped out in two days and for someone who otherwise has an active outdoor life, this feels amazing.

But this isn't new to me either. Although I haven't been completely off the grid for an entire weekend before, I have (every now and then) excused myself from socializing and instead enjoyed my own company. I've been doing this for a few years, and by now my loved ones understand that this way of being is an inherent part of my lifestyle.

Now, I must admit that I am privileged in ways that can make this happen. I don't work on weekends and so can do what I want to do during that time. I don't have anyone who's physically dependent on me and, therefore, can go invisible for a few days. I recognize these privileges and leverage them to set social boundaries and achieve goals.

Setting healthy social boundaries

I've set boundaries within a framework of things that I accept and want in my life. I'm flexible too and alter them to suit changing situations every once in a while. I've done so for many years now and swear by their life-transforming benefits. It's helped me be more authentic and has invited experiences that bring purpose and meaning to my life.

It starts when you learn to say no

If you are serious about cutting out the unnecessary so as to focus on projects that matter, you need to practice setting boundaries and saying no. It's a skill you have to learn, because it's not as straightforward as simply thinking or saying the words. It's a nuanced model — you need to say it with grace and ease, in a way that is firm but polite. You need to mean it and stick to it despite any temptations. Getting there takes time and patience, but once you do, you'll realize how purposeful you'll actually be. In this chapter, I will share with you some effective ways to say no and set boundaries. They work like magic.

You have privileges and priorities, so use them

We all have some privileges. Yours might be similar to or different from mine, but you have them nonetheless. Identify them and use them to help you achieve something you want for yourself. Likewise, identify your priorities and use the reasons to decline what could otherwise seem like an obligation.

You don't have to accept every invitation, nor be privy to gossip in your community

Let's face it; there will always be events to attend and invites to accept. Being part of society immediately puts you at the center of this system. But there will always be ways to turn them down in exchange for something more meaningful. Reflect on the invite or conversation. Does it give you happiness? Will it contribute to your knowledge? Is there something better you want to do? Someone else you want to spend your time with? If you think you'd rather be somewhere else doing something else, then you need to say no.

Try:

- "I can't go to the movies this weekend. I'm working on my book and have a deadline to keep." This prioritizes a purposeful activity that's time-bound.
- "I'd love to, but I'm busy that day. Have a good time." This is simple and to the point. If you don't have a reason to give, don't try and form one, because when you do, you don't sound convincing and that can get awkward.
- "Thanks for the invite, but it's during my gym time." After all, by this point in this book you're likely a stickler for fitness and well-being.
- "I'm sorry but I can't join you. I'm trying to create more time for a project I'm very passionate about and this is during that time." Now, if you want to make it up to them, you can always suggest another weekend or month. That's only if you want to though.
- "You know, as much as I want to spend time with you, I don't like how you talk about others when they aren't around. Can we not do that please? I don't think its right to discuss someone else's personal stuff." By saying this, you're letting them know how you feel.
- "I'm sorry, but I don't drink. You guys carry on. I'll catch you at work again tomorrow." This sets a boundary between personal and professional life.

"If I didn't define myself for myself, I would be crunched into other people's fantasies for me and eaten alive." — **Audre Lorde**

Part of being authentic and minimalistic comes from a strong sense of self and fearlessness. If you know what you want and want to achieve it really bad, then you should be ready to face all odds to achieve it. Keep going back to your belief system, and use it as a guiding anchor for your choices.

Likewise, don't let fear control you. When you begin to say no, you'll have apprehensions about how you will be received by people. Questions such as whether you will miss out are bound to cross your mind.

You may also wonder whether you'll stay relevant. Will people hate you if you say no too many times? What if people don't like you? What if you have no friends soon? How will you hold up? Let them be. Simply observe these thoughts and let them pass. These feelings will settle down over time and will disappear when you start using your time purposefully on dream projects.

The action of actually working on your goals will replace feelings of fear and guilt with feelings of satisfaction and contentment. You'll be your happiest self — the best version of you. You'll begin to smile more and will spend the little time you socialize meaningfully. And when you do all that, you'll radiate positivity and attract others who genuinely like you. You won't lose out on friends. If anything, you'll invite a clan of like-minded soul mates.

Points to remember

- Set healthy social boundaries. Learn to say no when you mean no.
- Reduce projects. Only work on things that you connect with and know can bring meaning to your life.
- Minimize events. Avoid attending events that you know can do harm to you. Instead, focus on surrounding yourself with projects and people that can help you. Also, look out for ways to contribute to projects and people's upliftment.

CHALLENGE TIME

Think about what an entire weekend of being with yourself and doing only what you want to do would be like. My guess? One word: bliss!

Here's something to get you started right away. Once a month have a no-texting-weekend. Simply tell those closest to you that you are safe and will not be available until Monday morning.

This only works if you're single and/or live alone. If you live with others, like many of us, cutting the digital chatter helps you to focus in on yourself with the added support of your loved ones. Inform them that you'll be having periodic 'me time' throughout the weekend.

PART 5 — ENVIRONMENT

CHAPTER 16 — TIDYING UP YOUR HOME

"The objective of cleaning is not just to clean, but to feel happiness living within that environment." — ***Marie Kondo***

As a society, an increasing number of people have more stuff than ever before. Their houses are bigger; they therefore have more things to fit inside it. Their garages are bigger and are mostly full of stuff that they don't use or rarely use. There is an entire society of individuals who live by the rule that more is never enough. With plenty accumulating endlessly on the side, they continue to buy, hoard, and show the many possessions they own.

Multiple industries are pushing this concept and are only too eager to help people deal with this clutter. From award-winning organizing solutions to storage units that allow you to hoard even more, sadly there are plenty of options to tuck away the filth that one wants to bring inside their homes and lives.

Clutter is disturbing and it can hurt you

At the minimum, all this clutter and extra stuff can be very distracting. When you have a pile of stuff in front of you, it becomes very difficult to ignore and instead fully focus on projects that matter. The idea that it's just sitting there, haphazardly and without any purpose, can easily consume your attention. So instead of thinking about ways to move your dream project ahead, your mind ends up going back to the clutter, wondering what you can do with it.

Even when it isn't in front you, the thought of the clutter can linger on and continue to distract. You may be away or might think you're not noticing it, but somewhere in the corner, your mind continues to chew on ways to get around it. Clutter can keep you from moving on and moving ahead. It can hold you captive when you want to get out. Clutter can be very disturbing and can hurt you when you least expect it.

Physical clutter negatively affects your ability to focus and process information

Scientists from the Princeton University Neuroscience Institute circulated the results of a study[48] they conducted in the January edition of *The Journal of Neuroscience*. The journal refers directly to uncluttered and organized living. The results describe how your surroundings play an important role in your state of mind. It explains how living in a cluttered environment can restrict your ability to focus, leaving you feeling distracted, irritable and less productive. It further explains how uncluttered or organized spaces can accentuate your mood, help you focus better, and help you be more productive.

My journey to declutter, organize, and live

As someone who likes to do away with any excess, I find myself cleaning through my living spaces from time to time. I've been doing this for some time now and I'm happy to say that I'm at a place where I don't accumulate much and, therefore, don't need a lot of time to tidy up. Getting here took time because, as mindful as I thought I was, somehow there would always be some pens that I wasn't using and other little knickknacks (mostly gifts) that would find their way into my space.

Things continue to accumulate (and they always will), but I don't let them sit in my place for long. I know what I have and know what I need and this makes identifying and getting rid of any extras easier for me.

I reach out to experts for inspiration

Tidying expert Marie Kondo has constructed a decluttering empire over time — first as a tidying consultant and then as an author of two bestselling books about her KonMari[49] decluttering process. Her KonMari method shows you how to organize your belongings as well as change your perception about things that you own, including yourself, your possessions, and the people you care about. Her tips are incredibly inspirational.

Stop subscribing to the one-in-one-out policy

Decluttering is a waste of time if you are guilty of mindlessly replacing things. The freedom from the desire to acquire is beautiful as it is liberating. Buy less, lend some, and borrow if you really need to. Slow the flow of letting things inside your home.

Get rid of at least one item in a week

Declutter one item from your house every week. To begin with, these can be obvious things such as excessive books and knickknacks/trinkets, but as time goes by and you possess less, you'll have to really think about what's sitting inside your drawers and hidden spaces. That's when you'll truly start decluttering. That's also when you'll begin to see it as a way of life.

Go through the list

Start with the obvious: letters, knickknacks/trinkets, household cleaning products, utensils, pots/pans, different sets of cutlery and dining ware (there's always a few more than we actually need). I've shared a detailed list at the end of this book which you can use as a guide to begin with. Go through your list and get rid of anything that seems extra and unnecessary.

Do not over-stock

A functional home doesn't need five extra pairs of linen, extra crockery, and extra pantry supplies. You don't need to stock up on toothbrushes, toiletries, and garbage bags (yes, even that too) just because they are on sale. Be realistic and only stock what you need for a month. In the event that someone does pop over, you can always borrow from loved ones or neighbors, or buy what you need just before they arrive.

Have a disposal plan

Before you go about getting rid of things, sit down and reflect on your life and your needs. Investigate your options to declutter. Can you sell something? How about recycling, donating, or giving it away to someone who might need it? The more thorough your plan is, the easier decluttering is.

Practice having a designated spot for everything

Choose a place to keep a thing, or a group of things, and stick to it, no matter what. The keys go into one place, the letters in another, and so on and so forth. Train your mind to ceremoniously keep them where they belong and, in time, you'll become habituated to it. As a result, nothing will ever go missing and it will save you the trouble and time to search for things.

Don't let clutter take over your life

Don't let clutter spoil what could otherwise be a loving, giving, and lively space. Every item you own occupies space in your house. Take time to manage your home, clean it, and repair it. Let your home be an extension of your thoughts. Let it be clear and positive, loving and purposeful.

Points to remember

- Stop subscribing to the one-in-one-out policy. Buy less, lend some, and borrow if you really need to.
- Do not over-stock.
- Have a disposal plan.
- Practice having a designated spot for everything.

CHALLENGE TIME

Dedicate an entire day or two or even a whole week to do a massive clean out of items. Separate the things you need and the things you don't really need. Soon you will consistently find that you won't need to clean as often as you currently do.

CHAPTER 17 — TIDYING OTHER PLACES: YOUR DESK AND CAR

"It's only after we've lost everything that we're free to do anything." — ***Tyler Durden, Fight Club***

Embracing minimalism as a way of living

When you begin decluttering, you'll realize the massive benefits you gain out of it. As a result of this one change, you'll find yourself being more composed and productive and feeling more centered and aware. You'll also be happier and will begin to enjoy your way of life. When that happens, you won't be able to help but keep things uncluttered and in order. Everything you own will have a purpose and a place of importance. Every space you take up will be exactly how you want it to be.

Defining your workplace

William is an architect who is loved for his minimalistic designs. He has this to say about how he defines his work: "My work is my passion project. It is my sanctity. It's something that I look forward to doing when I go to bed at night and something that I thoroughly enjoy while I'm at it. Having consciously sought a career that brings more of me into what I do, I feel naturally drawn to the things I work on. Work keeps me energized, keeps me happy."

How do you use minimalism in your work?

In response to this, William states, "I love playing with straight and horizontal lines. I also love to work on free-flowing curves as I think they somewhat connect to a lot in nature — mountains, landscapes, rivers and oceans, waves. I endorse the concept of less is more and love to explore my fascination for these forms in my designs. I mostly stick to one form or the other and use white spaces to balance things out."

How do you use minimalism in your workplace?

"Being a stickler for cleanliness and order," William says, "I like to keep my desk at work simple and functional. And because I spend most of my time there, I like to keep a few things that remind me of why I do what I do.

"Having experimented a bit, I now have a desk that suits my needs like a glove. A single-length wall-mounted desk that faces the window and opens to the wonderful view of a lush garden that sits below cleverly concealed drawers and open bookshelves. It's got everything I'll ever need — my laptop, books, paperwork, an indoor bamboo plant that I've nurtured and cared for over many years, and some other essentials. Everything has a place of its own and doesn't overcrowd each other. My desk is a living, breathing extension of my mindset and my home away from home. It is what helps me create the spaces I envision.

"Over the years of exploring, learning, and practicing this [minimalism], I've come up with ways to keep my surroundings exactly how I like them to be — functional, aesthetic, and uncluttered," he says.

In this chapter, I will share his best practices with you.

Golden rules for decluttering your desk at work

Let's start with paperwork. When you're talking about decluttering your desk at work, you'll always have plenty of paperwork around you. Work piece by piece and categorize what you want to do with them.

- File everything that is important and that you need to keep. Name the file appropriately and file everything that comes under it.

- Shred all sensitive information that you no longer need.
- Recycle everything else.

Moving on to drawers

Look at what sits inside these little spaces. Only keep what you use and need and throw away everything that doesn't have purpose.

Shelves

Label shelves based on the things you'd like to store in them. Place everything exactly where it belongs, making sure you place things that you use the most closer to where you sit.

Make a list

I recommend creating a list of the things you own along with the places you store them in (feel free to draw tips from the list I've shared at the end of this book). Refer to this list from time to time. Is everything in place? If it is not, then you know exactly what is missing and where it should be.

Organize everything else that sits on your desk

Organize your desk supplies from time to time. The markers (you don't need that many), notes, and clips all need a tiny little space for themselves. Again, compartmentalize and label them accordingly.

De-junk the junk drawers

Yes, you have them. Go through the drawers in which you conveniently shove everything else. Get rid of things that are merely eating space. Now, this goes well for your house. So, go ahead and apply them wherever you choose to.

Move onto other spaces

There is no shortcut to cleanliness and order. It takes discipline and consistency. But the beauty of decluttering is that the more you do it, the more you are surrounded with only the things you love and need. With all this positivity on your side, you'll have what it takes to keep at it.

Decluttering your car

Just as you make decluttering a way of life and go about tidying up your environment, you might want to shift your focus to your mode of transport.

When you begin to live inside your car

To some, their mode of transport becomes an extension of their homes. As a result, in pursuit of being prepared, they carry enough supplies to live inside it. While it's alright to carry a set of gym clothes while on the go and on the way to the gym, carrying more can be avoided (unless you are living in your car, in which case, it is totally understandable and okay).

Ways to keep your car clean and organized

First, assess what you genuinely need to have on hand while on the road. Don't include things that fall into the 'just in case' category. Instead, only think about the absolute essentials — things you might need in case of an emergency.

Next, empty everything that currently lives inside your car, giving it a wash down while you are at it. Seeing your car clean and organized might make it difficult for you to clutter, especially if you've gone through the pain of tidying it up yourself. Once you've given it a good scrub, re-evaluate everything you need and only keep the absolute essentials.

Throw out garbage

Your living spaces, and by that I mean any space you spend any time in, is an extension of who you are as a person and what you think. Having a cluttered space, in this case your car, can mean you have a lot of inner chatter in your head. It can also mean that you are insensitive to mess and the ill-effects of it on society and the environment at large. If you want to live healthily and think positively, start by acting like you mean good. Hoarding garbage and left-over food inside the car is unhygienic in every way. So, throw out garbage including any old gas and petrol receipts. If you need the bills for some reason, file them once you reach home.

Only keep the essentials in the trunk

You don't need a closet full of clothes in the trunk, just the essentials. Revisit this list every day and replace it with relevant stuff for that day. My essentials include a first aid kit, a pair of shoes, and a jacket.

Leave the dashboard alone

Because the dashboard is so close to the windscreen of your car, cluttering your dashboard with things can become a reason for distraction. My suggestion is to limit the number of things you keep on your dashboard. That way, you're more likely to have a clearer line of sight and can focus on your driving better.

Points to remember

- Go through your paperwork. File what is important, shred what is sensitive, and recycle everything else.
- Create labels and list the things you own along with where you can find them.
- Get rid of clutter in your car every day.
- Avoid cluttering the dashboard and keep only the essentials in the trunk.

CHALLENGE TIME

- Get rid of clutter every day. Get rid of garbage that accumulates on your desk and in your car on a daily basis. The more diligent you are with this, the less you pile up, and the more organized your desk at work will be.

PART 6 — MONEY

CHAPTER 18 — CUTTING OUT NON-ESSENTIALS TO SAVE

"Too many people spend money they earned to buy things they don't want to impress people that they don't like." — **Will Rogers**

Back in the day, when I was just starting out, I didn't have a lot of money and was trying to understand what money meant to me and whether or not I wanted to spend my life chasing it. I realized that I wanted money, but not as a means to go after luxuries and possessions, but as a means to live life simply and in a way that gave me happiness.

I need money, but I am not the contents of my wallet. I need money to live and go through the basic routines of life. I like to travel and collect experiences, and so I need money to help me do just that. I realized that what is more important than my income is how I spend the resources I have. Because despite the income I draw, there will always be certain things that I cannot buy. The point is whether I want to buy them? More importantly, whether I need them in life? I choose to place need over everything else. I earn enough. I live within my means, I live deliberately, and I'm very happy. When I realized this, I decided to take control of my finances and my life. I remember taking certain decisions (and they mostly remain the same principles, even today) that helped me save and experience life in the way I want to.

"The greatest wealth is to live content with your life." — **Plato**

Real wealth, assurance, and happiness come not from the charms we amass, but from how we spend the one life we've been gifted. Taking control over your finances can be daunting at first — particularly due to the present self-indulgent culture we live amongst — but it is easier than you think. Recovering control of your expenditure and savings can actually be simple, provided that you are willing to look inside, change your financial habits, work within the resources you have, and be minimalistic.

Why?

Minimalism doesn't mean you strip yourself of everything you love and need. Definitely not, because that's not living. Minimalism is about buying what you need and not what you desire and there is a massive difference between the two. It's about asking why before you buy.

For instance, I love cars but why do I need to own one? And if I do, why a particular kind of car? If its only purpose is to move me from place to place, then why do I need to spend all that money on something that is going to depreciate in time just because it is fancy? Now, these questions can be different for different people and rely on context. For instance, if you live in a place where the weather demands you invest in anti-skid tires or something similar, then by all means you must purchase these. Likewise, if public transport is not the best option for you, then yes, investing in a good car might be the best way out.

The point I'm trying to make here is to put need before everything else. If you believe you need something, then you should definitely invest your money in acquiring it. But if you don't, then ask yourself a few questions before reaching an answer, such as whether you want to subscribe to this model. Is there a better way out? How can you use your money more mindfully?

Questions such as these will ultimately lead you to the right decisions. They'll move from questioning why you need a fancy car to other unnecessary things, such as an extra pair of shoes, that fancy coffee mug, an additional couch for invisible guests, etc. Minimalism will save you money by getting rid of excess, spending less overall, and spending mindfully when you do so. So always ask why.

Budget

Most of us have no idea where our money is going. We think we know but we don't really know. Having a written budget will help you understand what you have to work with. It will help set boundaries.

Categorize

Identify everything that you need. Divide your list into essentials, non-essentials, and junk. Note down every expense (food, clothing, accommodation, utilities, insurance, vehicles, gas, transportation, credit cards, phones, internet, pets, fun, etc.). Now, go through your list twice over to bookmark only the things you need. Stay strict and only select the essentials. The more mindful you are, the sooner you will be free.

Buy what lasts

Some items are meant to perish. Food is one such thing- it has a shorter expiry date — but most of the big purchases in life are meant to last a long time. Focus on quality over quantity and value for money over something cheap and thrift. Focus on longevity over something that is seasonal. Occasionally, doing this might mean you end up spending a little more initially, but that's okay. The purchase will save you money in the long run. The idea is not to avoid spending money or be frugal, but to rather spend money on things that last.

If you have thrown it out once, will you buy it again?

So often, we discard things because they've been irrelevant and buy them back at another time simply because we continue to feel attracted to it. It doesn't have purpose in our lives, and probably never will, but we buy it anyway because we feel drawn to it. Well, it's time to change your mindset. Only buy things that you need and that you know you will use.

Minimize

Minimalism is not about deprivation. I don't want to live with the feeling of being deprived, or want anyone else to live like that. However, simplifying can add value to your life and can help you save big.

Contribute, donate, gift, sell

If you have something that doesn't add value to you and your life but you know it could be useful to a friend, gift it away. If, however, you don't know of anyone who can use it, donate it. And if you think it can fetch you good money, then put it up on sale.

Stay content

The surest route towards freedom is the path of happiness and contentment. It is the state of mind where you are happy with where you are and with what you have. Appreciate your present and feel grateful for the gifts you already have. And if there is still something that you want from life, then work your way towards achieving it mindfully and without the excess.

Simple isn't easy

Living simply while following a minimalist lifestyle isn't easy, but then again, you probably knew that before you read this chapter. But it isn't that daunting either. Over the course of being mindful and minimalistic, you'll soon realize you've always lived quite simply, but you might only just realize it now.

Points to remember

- When it comes to spending money, put need before everything else.
- Having a written budget will help you understand what you have to work with. It will help set boundaries.
- Quality trumps everything.
- Be mindful of your needs. Stay mindful of your expenditure.

CHALLENGE TIME

Keep aside some money as savings every month. It might help if you create a budget for this. So every month, before you allow yourself to spend money, set aside some cash as savings. Do not touch that money so as to allow it to multiply quickly.

CHAPTER 19 — PLANNING WHAT YOU SPEND AHEAD OF TIME

"Plan your work and work your plan." — **Napoleon Hill**

Since moving out of the comfort of my parent's home, I've come to realize the value of money. Every luxury that I had and perhaps took for granted wasn't easily available soon after I left the nest. I've had to earn my way and I'm glad I've come this far. I work very hard and don't want to put my hard work to waste. I always look for value and necessity before making a purchase and am always on the lookout for ways to use less.

I've learned a lesson or two about savings since then. I now know that saving doesn't merely mean putting a portion of my earnings into bank accounts. Saving to me is about buying and consuming only what I need. It's about planning ahead and looking for deals that give me value for money. It's about placing quality over quantity and momentary satisfaction, because quality trumps everything and translates to savings in the long run. I now think long-term and don't buckle to impulses.

Through understanding my relationship with money over the years, I've reflected, explored, learned, stumbled, regained, and triumphed. This experience has allowed me to come up with money-saving strategies that, while in-line with my minimalistic life goals, make saving a little easier for me. In this chapter, I will share some of my best practices with you.

*"To be smart enough to get all that money you must be dull enough to want it." — **Gilbert Keith Chesterton***

Make a list of impulse-purchase regrets

I cannot emphasize just how useful these lists are. I have one for my essentials, non-essentials, and any indulgences. I also have one that consists of any impulse-purchase regrets.

If you've ever bought something and later regretted it, put that down. And if you ever went, "What was I thinking?" well then, that too. These little notes tell a story. They give you a glimpse of your triggers and show you a pattern to the impulse shopping you do. Knowing how you spend your money is great, but knowing when you've done it out of impulse is even better. It will help you address and eliminate the habit once and for all.

Spend less time browsing and avoid going to the mall

If you know that you have little control over your impulse urges, then avoid creating situations that might tempt you to spend. For example, avoid going to the mall unless it's necessary, such as if there is a great deal on something you need and it's only available in the retail store at the mall. Also, reduce the time you spend on browsing, especially on online retail websites. Unsubscribe from store emails as they tend to pop up every day and can tempt you into unnecessarily spending.

Plan ahead and buy when the time's right

While this might sound time-consuming to some, planning ahead is one of the most effective ways to curtail and save. If you have to make a purchase, make a list of things you need to buy; club them together as you might luck out on discounts and free shipping options when you buy more. Use online shopping to buy things that will save you money and time. There are plenty of deals online, and when you need to make a purchase, this can come very handy. I recommend that you use it to your advantage, but make sure you aren't redeeming every other offer when you don't need to.

Refer to your budget and spending goals

Again, make a list of short-term and long-term goals and ask yourself how this potential purchase might influence your goals. The rule of thumb is to always keep a mental and physical note of your financial goals, including your monthly commitments, debts, and savings. Refer to this note before any purchase. Ask yourself:

- Does this purchase fit into my budget?
- Will this purchase improve my quality of life?
- Do I already have this item or something similar to this at home?
- Why do I really want this item?

If the results aren't harmful and the purchase justified, then by all means, go for it. But if they are not, then you'll have to put it in your wish list for another day and another time. The good thing is that if you really want it, you can work hard to save up and buy it.

Be mindful of your tribe

It is said that you are the average of the people you spend most of your time with. Irrespective of how disciplined and self-assured you are, your close relationships can influence how you think and act and how you spend and shop. So choose wisely.

Transact with cash and debit cards wherever possible

Transacting with cash and debits is far safer and more controlled than transacting with credit cards. (1) The money is yours and you, therefore, become more conscious of the fact that you are spending your hard-earned money. (2) The money has a limit, meaning you can't go beyond your means.

Do your best to save

Saving is never easy. It takes discipline, consistent planning, and a lot of hard work, but it is possible. Every little bit counts. Just start saving without spending too much time on whether you can or not. The key is to start soon. How about now?

When in doubt, use minimalism as a tool to remind you of your personal values

Once you embrace minimalism as a way of life, you'll notice how it will seamlessly seep into every aspect of your life. As a result of my choices, I am more focused on what I desire, envision, attract, and invite into my life. This shift has made me become more mindful in everything I do. I always have my largest priorities in mind and make an effort into actually bringing them to play. They define the framework within which I make my choices and live my life and I rarely do something without knowing why I am doing it. Minimalism helps me live purposefully. As a result, I spend money purposefully and not accidentally.

Points to remember

- Know your splurging patterns. Make a list of impulse-purchase regrets.
- Spend less time browsing and avoid going to the mall.
- Plan ahead and buy when the time is right.
- Refer to your budget and spending goals.
- Transact with cash and debit cards wherever possible.
- Start saving now.

CHALLENGE TIME

- Plan to exercise 'no spend days/week' and see how much you have saved by the end by simply not touching your wallet. Rest assured, you'll be taken in by the results.

PART 7 — FREEDOM

CHAPTER 20 — TRAVELING LIGHT

"Simplicity is making the journey of this life with just baggage enough." — **Charles Dudley Warner**

I love exploring new locations, meeting new people, learning new languages, and understanding new cultures. The diversity makes me feel strangely connected, like we are all different but one. Part of why I love minimalism so much is because it helps me to do the stuff that I love in the most natural and simple way.

When I decided to have less stuff, I didn't realize the effect of the change I'd be inviting into my life. Having less means I have more time and money to travel. Now, this could be different for others, but there is a good reason why travel and minimalism get mentioned in the same breath. When you begin to prioritize and downsize, you have less things to weigh you down and more time, energy, and resources to spend on experiences that matter — travel helps me realize those experiences.

But travel, however well thought out, is no small feat for anyone. One minute you can think you have everything going according to plan, and in the next, you're thrown on the opposite side from where you started. It takes planning, preparing, and then being ready to drop it all to go with the flow. Furthermore, no matter where you decide to go, travel will never be cheap, which is another reason why it requires careful planning. Because I love and do it so much, I like to do whatever I can to lower the pitfalls (and there will be a few along the way).

I asked a few fellow travelers about their best practices while traveling. Here are their answers.

I turn to minimalism

"It helps that, when I'm not traveling, I work very hard on projects that matter to me the most," says Dorothy, a freelance writer. "I rarely eat out, don't buy out of a whim, and am very mindful of what I spend my money on. I value my time and try and make it work for me.

"I love to experience, learn, and share just as I love to write. And so, I write even while I'm traveling, meaning I keep the workflow and income steady. Because I do what I love to do, I thrive on it. I'm happy and can keep going.

"I try and spend my money purposefully and save as much of that money for travel. It also helps that I don't replace things easily, usually preferring to repair any broken item until it gets to a point where it isn't functional. I buy less, but buy stuff of high quality. So you see, by just doing the basics and doing it right, I'm able to live my dreams and travel at my will," she concludes.

Travel light

Kieran, an avid traveler and my go-to person for destination advice, shares his tips on traveling light. "I'm not a big fan of airports," he says. "I don't like lugging luggage around and therefore have mastered the art of packing only carry-on luggage. All I need are a few essentials and I'm good to go. Again, it's all about finding the right things and putting them together. Over the years, I've invested in some high-quality travel essentials that are built to endure. And because I travel so much, they are worth their dime. Irrespective of how long my trip is, my go-to kit consists of a high-quality duffle bag that is light, but has ample storage."

Here's what he packs inside it:

- A few tops that are season friendly (usually monochrome colors)
- A pair of jeans plus another one that I wear while traveling
- Innerwear

- A small drying towel
- An extra pair of socks
- Toiletries
- Chargers for my phone and camera

"They fit snugly into my bag and are just right to get going. I feel freer and am guaranteed a hassle-free airport commute. Perfect! Now I obviously also carry my phone and camera, but I usually have them on me so it doesn't occupy much space," he concludes.

Travel to places you want to go to

Richa, a friend I made on one of my trips, loves to travel too. She works in the banking industry and believes her hectic schedules have taught her to plan in advance. "Like everything else in my life," she says, "I decide where, when, and how I travel. This allows me to be flexible and make the most of the off-season rates. Besides, I don't go places just because it's the most visited. I shape my travel according to my interests and, therefore, I'm able to soak in the beauty of exploring some unknowns."

Having fewer possessions means you don't leave too much behind

Having traveled a bit myself, I completely agree with Dorothy, Kieran, and Richa. I also feel that when you don't amass much, you don't have to worry about leaving things behind when you're away traveling. This is a huge bonus in my opinion. With nothing to fear or worry about, I spend all my attention on the one thing I love the most: travel.

Blend in

As most travelers will tell you, the real experience of travel comes from living the life of the locals. I'm no different. I like to keep things real and try to blend in with the crowd. That said, I suggest you first do a little homework. Always learn a thing or two about the place and the culture you are about to witness. Reading helps you to achieve that to some extent, but don't get too bogged down with expectations. Leave a little room for discovering a surprise.

Here are some of my best practices on blending in:

- Observe as well as talk to the locals.
- Sink into the experience.
- You don't have to take every photo and be in every frame.
- Collect memories by experiencing and living in the moment.
- Blend and become one with the new world so that when you are ready to return, you can carry the memories and lessons from the eventful experience

Points to remember

- Travel light.
- Travel to places you want to go.
- Having fewer possessions means you don't leave too much behind.
- For a real experience, blend in with the locals. Live their life, and walk their walk.

CHALLENGE TIME

- If you have the funds, book a solo trip in the next four months. You will never be the same. But if you fear solo travel, try semi-solo travel by booking with a tour group. Begin your homework and challenge yourself to book within the next two weeks. I know it's scary, but I ask you to trust me on this. Close your eyes figuratively, book it, and don't look back. You can thank me later.

"Our freedom corresponds directly with our ability to walk away from anything." — ***Joshua Fields Millburn***

CHAPTER 21 — LIVING WITH PASSION

"Passion is energy. Feel the power that comes from focusing on what excites you." — **Oprah Winfrey**

Some people live their lives with passion and purpose as a way to be happy. I am no different. I like to read and grow my knowledge. I like to reflect on what I read to see if it makes sense in my life. And if it does, I like to apply it to my circle of experiences in a way that it aligns with my passion and brings me happiness. Through it all, I also hope to understand a little more of me.

A few years ago, I came across three minimalistic Japanese concepts that stuck with me.

Fumio Asaki, an enlightened minimalism expert, promotes the concept of Danshari in his book, *Goodbye, Things*[50]. Danshari (also referred to as the art of decluttering, discarding, and parting with your possessions) is explained with three ideograms: refuse, dispose, and separate. Three simple words but which provide a wealth of insight.

- *R*efuse to bring unnecessary new possessions into your life.
- *Dispose* of existing clutter in your living space.
- *S*eparate from a desire for material possessions.

Another concept is Ikigai[51], which translates to reason for life and talks about putting deep reflection into your wants and needs in all areas of your life. It advocates finding reason in doing:

- what you love (passion and mission)
- what you are good at (passion and profession)

- what you can be paid for (profession and vocation)
- what the world needs (mission and vocation)

Additionally, Wabi-Sabi[52], a Zen philosophy, talks about accepting yourself as you truly are — with your imperfections too — and believing that you are beautiful. While this, much like the other two philosophies, speaks about understated elegance and focuses on the less-is-more mentality, Wabi-Sabi is also about taking pleasure in the imperfect.

I find these concepts extremely relevant and believe they can be applied to every aspect of life, including finding and living your passion. Due to their wealth of insight, I keep going back to them and find that my understanding of them and myself have evolved over time and across circumstances. So will yours as you begin to implement their lessons.

Path to passion

Some people go through life believing the job they have is the career they will have until they retire one day. Despite any conflicts, they adjust, adapt, compromise, sacrifice, grumble, and succumb to a particular lifestyle; a lifestyle that is based on what others think is great. They spend, borrow, and consume much to live this life. They then get stuck in this web, and before they even realize it, have invested so much of themselves and are so high up the ladder that stepping down and starting afresh is an unthinkable proposition. And so, they keep inching along, pretending they are happy when they are not. They fail to ask the important question simply because they fear they cannot act out the answer.

At the outset, there is nothing wrong with living this way. But if you want to be authentic and want to experience something extraordinary, then you need to step back and really ask yourself whether you are happy. The answer might not surprise you, but it will definitely set the ball rolling. Once you begin asking the right questions, you'll discover yourself and your passion. And when you do that, when you find something (anything) that you're crazy passionate about, you'll find the strength to re-write your story but this time with conviction and joy.

There will be small losses along the way, but they'll be lessons too, and through it all you'll find a reward like nothing else. You no longer will be merely earning a paycheck, but will be earning your life back. You'll be your authentic self, working on passion projects and living the life of your dreams. From personal experience, I can tell you that the experience is enriching to say the least.

My passion project involves the written work I do. What does yours look like?

While recognizing your passion is a major leap ahead, it is only the beginning of a rewarding journey. Backed with passion, you must now act out your purpose. My two cents are to follow the principles of minimalism.

Keep it simple

The thing about most people is that they spend their entire lives chasing a life that they aren't convinced or happy about and plead for an opportunity to set things right. However, when the opportunity comes knocking at their door, they speculate, procrastinate, and actually excuse themselves from walking the walk. They miss the bus and continue to plead for a second chance, and a third, and a fourth....

Don't give yourself another reason to delay things again. When it comes to making second chances count, you want to dive straight in and keep the plan simple and straightforward.

Stop trying and start doing

- Are you *trying* to be more authentic? Stop *trying*. Start *being*.
- Are you *trying* to cut back on technology? Stop *trying*. Start *deleting*.
- Are you *trying* to simplify your life? Stop *trying*. Start *decluttering*.

- Are you *trying* to start healthy mind-stimulating routines? Stop *trying*. Start *meditating*.
- Are you *trying* to control your environment? Stop *trying*. Start *minimizing*.
- Are you *trying* to gain better control over your finances? Stop *trying*. Start *saving*.
- Are you trying to find your passion? Stop trying. Start asking the *right questions*.

Points to remember

Practice Danshari:

- *R*efuse to bring unnecessary new possessions into your life.
- *T*hrow away existing clutter in your living space.
- *S*eparate from a desire for material possessions.

Practice Ikigai and discover:

- what you love (passion and mission)
- what you are good at (passion and profession)
- what you can be paid for (profession and vocation)
- what the world needs (mission and vocation)

Practice Wabi-Sabi by accepting yourself as you truly are, including your imperfections.

CHALLENGE TIME

Using the insights presented in this book as well as your own judgment, live with less and pursue your passions.

Starting now, focus on ways you can:

- Live with less while spending more time on meaningful projects.
- Live with less while exploring the freedom to travel and move about.
- Live with less while gaining more clarity about your spiritual pursuits.

- Live with less while having more control over your thoughts and actions, and mental and physical self.
- Live with less while being the best version of yourself on any given day.

"Your time is limited, so don't waste it living someone else's life." — ***Steve Jobs***

CONCLUSION

Contributing to a better world

Seeing that the majority of the world doesn't have it all together and has to work very hard (including myself) to get what they want in life has taught me to see life in a new way. I now value everything that I have and don't take them for granted. I'm also very grateful for everything that I have and try not to ask for more than I need (and I consciously have to work at realizing this).

I believe if people become more conscious of what they spend money on and how they use the stuff they own (by valuing and conserving everything), the world can be a better place. The conscious changes I've made to my approach towards life have helped me tremendously. I believe they can help you too. I also believe that everyone is capable of being as happy as I am today. I want to help you because I care for you. I've had an enriching experience writing this book and hope that comes through to you as you read it.

You are here and today is a great day to start

As we reach the end of this book, I urge you to reflect on everything that exists within these pages and use them to embrace a more focused approach to life. I urge you to really think about every decision and indecision, every step you take forward and every step you retreat, every time you have been authentic and every time you have not. I ask you to think about these because they brought you to where you stand today. Now that you are here, where do you want to go?

Now that you've made all those cuts, look at the time on your hands and use it to blossom into the new improved you: the minimalist babe.

LIST

MIND

DIGITAL	KEEP	MINIMIZE	THROW
Old e-Mails	☐	☐	☐
Selfies / Photo Multiples	☐	☐	☐
Movies	☐	☐	☐
Music	☐	☐	☐
Entertainment Subscriptions	☐	☐	☐
Old Files	☐	☐	☐
Unused Apps	☐	☐	☐
Social Media Followings	☐	☐	☐

EDUCATIONAL	KEEP	MINIMIZE	THROW
Adhesives	☐	☐	☐
Calculators	☐	☐	☐
Dried up Markers	☐	☐	☐
Extra Bookmarks	☐	☐	☐
Extra Pencil Sharpeners	☐	☐	☐
Old Backpack	☐	☐	☐
Old Books	☐	☐	☐
Old Notebooks	☐	☐	☐
Old Pencils, Erasers	☐	☐	☐
Rulers	☐	☐	☐

BODY

APPAREL	KEEP	MINIMIZE	THROW
Belts	☐	☐	☐
Boots	☐	☐	☐
Boxers / Briefs	☐	☐	☐
Bras	☐	☐	☐
Cufflinks	☐	☐	☐
Dresses	☐	☐	☐
Earrings	☐	☐	☐
Extra Shoelaces	☐	☐	☐
Flip Flops	☐	☐	☐
Glasses	☐	☐	☐
Gloves	☐	☐	☐
Halloween Costumes	☐	☐	☐
Hats	☐	☐	☐
Headbands	☐	☐	☐
High Heels	☐	☐	☐
Jackets / Coats	☐	☐	☐
Leggings	☐	☐	☐
Necklaces	☐	☐	☐
Pajamas	☐	☐	☐
Panties	☐	☐	☐
Pants	☐	☐	☐
Purses / Bags	☐	☐	☐

Rings	☐	☐	☐
Runner Shoes	☐	☐	☐
Scarves	☐	☐	☐
Shirts	☐	☐	☐
Shorts	☐	☐	☐
Skirts	☐	☐	☐
Sneakers	☐	☐	☐
Socks	☐	☐	☐
Sunglasses	☐	☐	☐
Sweaters / Hoodies	☐	☐	☐
Swimwear	☐	☐	☐
Tie / Bow Ties	☐	☐	☐
T-shirts	☐	☐	☐
Wallets	☐	☐	☐
Watches	☐	☐	☐

GROOMING	**KEEP**	**MINIMIZE**	**THROW**
Cologne / Perfume	☐	☐	☐
Curlers	☐	☐	☐
Eye Shadow Palettes	☐	☐	☐
False Lashes	☐	☐	☐
Foundation	☐	☐	☐
Foundation	☐	☐	☐
Glues	☐	☐	☐
Hair Clipper	☐	☐	☐
Hair Dryer	☐	☐	☐

Hair Dyes	☐	☐	☐
Hair Iron	☐	☐	☐
Hair Ties	☐	☐	☐
Highlighters	☐	☐	☐
Lip Balm	☐	☐	☐
Lip Gloss	☐	☐	☐
Lipstick	☐	☐	☐
Mascara	☐	☐	☐
Masks	☐	☐	☐
Nail Polish	☐	☐	☐
Nail Polish Remover	☐	☐	☐
Old Brushes	☐	☐	☐
Old DIY Products	☐	☐	☐
Old Makeup Sponges	☐	☐	☐
Pencils	☐	☐	☐
Powders	☐	☐	☐
Primer	☐	☐	☐
Shoe Polish	☐	☐	☐

HYGIENE	KEEP	MINIMIZE	THROW
Bath Salts / Bombs	☐	☐	☐
Bobby Pins	☐	☐	☐
Conditioner	☐	☐	☐
Contact Lens Cases	☐	☐	☐
Cotton Buds	☐	☐	☐

Creams & Lotions	☐	☐	☐
Deodorant	☐	☐	☐
Eye Drops	☐	☐	☐
Face Washes	☐	☐	☐
Feminine Products	☐	☐	☐
Floss	☐	☐	☐
Lotions	☐	☐	☐
Old Mouthwash	☐	☐	☐
Old Sexual Health Products	☐	☐	☐
Old Teeth Whitening Trays	☐	☐	☐
Shampoo	☐	☐	☐
Shaving Cream	☐	☐	☐
Shaving Sticks	☐	☐	☐
Soap	☐	☐	☐
Sunscreen	☐	☐	☐
Tissues	☐	☐	☐
Toothpaste	☐	☐	☐

SOUL

HABITS	KEEP	MINIMIZE	THROW
Drinking (Alcohol)	☐	☐	☐
Pessimism	☐	☐	☐
Procrastination	☐	☐	☐
Sedentary Lifestyle	☐	☐	☐
Smoking	☐	☐	☐
TV	☐	☐	☐

NETWORK	KEEP	MINIMIZE	THROW
Email Contacts	☐	☐	☐
Exes	☐	☐	☐
Phone Contacts	☐	☐	☐
Toxic People	☐	☐	☐

ENVIRONMENT

KITCHEN	KEEP	MINIMIZE	THROW
Blenders	☐	☐	☐
Bottle Openers	☐	☐	☐
Canned Goods	☐	☐	☐
Cereal Boxes	☐	☐	☐
Chipped Chinaware	☐	☐	☐
Coasters	☐	☐	☐
Cookbooks	☐	☐	☐
Cookie Cutters	☐	☐	☐
Damaged Plates, Cups and Mugs	☐	☐	☐
Deep Fryers	☐	☐	☐
Dishware	☐	☐	☐
Duplicate Measuring Cups	☐	☐	☐
Excess Shot Glasses	☐	☐	☐
Expired Coupons	☐	☐	☐
Expired Sauces	☐	☐	☐
Extra Cocktail Shakers	☐	☐	☐
Fondue Sets	☐	☐	☐
Fridge Magnets	☐	☐	☐
Kitchen Knives	☐	☐	☐
Kitchen Mats	☐	☐	☐
Kitchen Towels	☐	☐	☐
Loyalty Cards	☐	☐	☐

Mason Jars	☐	☐	☐
Old Napkins	☐	☐	☐
Old Paper Plates	☐	☐	☐
Old Spices	☐	☐	☐
Plastic Containers	☐	☐	☐
Plastic Grocery Bags	☐	☐	☐
Rice Cookers	☐	☐	☐
Scratched Pots and Pans	☐	☐	☐
Stale Pasta / Cereal / Crackers / Chips	☐	☐	☐
Tablecloths	☐	☐	☐
Takeout Chopsticks	☐	☐	☐
Toasters	☐	☐	☐
Twist Ties	☐	☐	☐
Unused Vases	☐	☐	☐
Wine / Liquor / Beer Bottles	☐	☐	☐

LIVING ROOM	KEEP	MINIMIZE	THROW
Board Games	☐	☐	☐
Blankets	☐	☐	☐
Letters	☐	☐	☐
Magazines	☐	☐	☐
Newspapers	☐	☐	☐
Old Air Fresheners	☐	☐	☐
Old Candles	☐	☐	☐
Old Curtains	☐	☐	☐

Pillows	☐	☐	☐
Plants	☐	☐	☐
Rugs	☐	☐	☐
Side Tables	☐	☐	☐
Unused Vases	☐	☐	☐

BEDROOM	**KEEP**	**MINIMIZE**	**THROW**
Alarm Clock	☐	☐	☐
Damaged Blankets	☐	☐	☐
Extra / Old Bed Linens	☐	☐	☐
Hangers	☐	☐	☐
Journals	☐	☐	☐
Misc. Bedside Table Items	☐	☐	☐
Night Lights	☐	☐	☐
Old Mattresses	☐	☐	☐
Old Pillows	☐	☐	☐
Storage Boxes	☐	☐	☐

BATHROOM	**KEEP**	**MINIMIZE**	**THROW**
Air Fresheners / Potpourri	☐	☐	☐
Bathmats	☐	☐	☐
Bleach	☐	☐	☐
Cleaning Gloves	☐	☐	☐
Cleaning Rags	☐	☐	☐
Cleaning Sprays	☐	☐	☐
Dispensers	☐	☐	☐

Glass Cleaner	☐	☐	☐
Loofahs and Sponges	☐	☐	☐
Old Shower Curtains	☐	☐	☐
Old Toilet Brushes	☐	☐	☐
Old Towels	☐	☐	☐

ELECTRONICS	**KEEP**	**MINIMIZE**	**THROW**
Bluetooth Speakers	☐	☐	☐
Cassette Tapes	☐	☐	☐
Disposable Cameras	☐	☐	☐
Duplicate USB Cables	☐	☐	☐
DVD & CD Cases	☐	☐	☐
DVD/Tape Players	☐	☐	☐
DVD's	☐	☐	☐
Earphones	☐	☐	☐
Excess Audio Video Cords	☐	☐	☐
External Hard Drives	☐	☐	☐
Extra Mice and Keyboards	☐	☐	☐
Game Consoles	☐	☐	☐
Landline Telephones	☐	☐	☐
Memory Cards	☐	☐	☐
Music CDs	☐	☐	☐
Old Cameras	☐	☐	☐
Old Laptops	☐	☐	☐
Old TV's	☐	☐	☐
Old Mobile Phones	☐	☐	☐

Phone Covers	☐	☐	☐
Printers	☐	☐	☐
Remote Controls	☐	☐	☐
Routers	☐	☐	☐
Unused Vacuums	☐	☐	☐
USB Drives	☐	☐	☐
Video Games	☐	☐	☐

DECOR	KEEP	MINIMIZE	THROW
Candles	☐	☐	☐
Empty Photo Albums	☐	☐	☐
Lamps	☐	☐	☐
Old Calendars	☐	☐	☐
Souvenirs	☐	☐	☐
Unused Picture Frames	☐	☐	☐
Wall Art	☐	☐	☐
Vases / Pots	☐	☐	☐

PARENTING	KEEP	MINIMIZE	THROW
Bibs	☐	☐	☐
Blankets	☐	☐	☐
Bottles	☐	☐	☐
Broken Toys	☐	☐	☐
Chairs / Transport	☐	☐	☐
Cribs	☐	☐	☐
Old School work	☐	☐	☐

Outgrown Books	☐	☐	☐
Outgrown Clothing	☐	☐	☐
Old Products	☐	☐	☐
Pacifiers	☐	☐	☐
Utensils	☐	☐	☐

FRONT / BACKYARD	KEEP	MINIMIZE	THROW
Dead Flowers / Plants	☐	☐	☐
Flowerpots	☐	☐	☐
Garden Decor	☐	☐	☐
Garden Hose	☐	☐	☐
Garden Shovels	☐	☐	☐
Pesticides / Herbicides	☐	☐	☐
Old Patio Furniture	☐	☐	☐
Watering Cans	☐	☐	☐

GARAGE	KEEP	MINIMIZE	THROW
Air Beds	☐	☐	☐
Brooms	☐	☐	☐
Bubble Wrap	☐	☐	☐
Camping Gear	☐	☐	☐
Car Supplies	☐	☐	☐
Cardboard Boxes	☐	☐	☐
Christmas Ornaments	☐	☐	☐
Duplicate Tools	☐	☐	☐
Exercise Equipment	☐	☐	☐

Flotation Devices	☐	☐	☐
Folding Chairs	☐	☐	☐
Holiday Lights	☐	☐	☐
Instruments	☐	☐	☐
Luggage Bags	☐	☐	☐
Mops	☐	☐	☐
Nuts, Screws and Bolts	☐	☐	☐
Old Bicycles	☐	☐	☐
Paint Containers	☐	☐	☐
Party Supplies	☐	☐	☐
Pet Toys	☐	☐	☐
Posters	☐	☐	☐
Scrap Wood	☐	☐	☐
Snow Shovels	☐	☐	☐
Sports Equipment	☐	☐	☐
Styrofoam Packing	☐	☐	☐
Tape Measures	☐	☐	☐
Tires	☐	☐	☐
Tools	☐	☐	☐
Umbrellas	☐	☐	☐
Unusable Paint Brushes	☐	☐	☐

CAR	**KEEP**	**MINIMIZE**	**THROW**
Broken Navigation System	☐	☐	☐
Cup holders	☐	☐	☐
Expired First Aid Kit	☐	☐	☐

Extra Clothing	☐	☐	☐
Food Leftovers	☐	☐	☐
Nik-Naks	☐	☐	☐
Old Ashtray	☐	☐	☐
Old Floor Mats	☐	☐	☐
Ripped Seat Covers	☐	☐	☐
Unused Tools	☐	☐	☐

WORK DESK	**KEEP**	**MINIMIZE**	**THROW**
Binders, Folders and Portfolios	☐	☐	☐
Blunt Scissors	☐	☐	☐
Business Cards	☐	☐	☐
Calendars	☐	☐	☐
Catalogues	☐	☐	☐
Computer Software CDs	☐	☐	☐
Day Planners	☐	☐	☐
Greeting Cards	☐	☐	☐
Highlighters	☐	☐	☐
Magazines	☐	☐	☐
Mouse Pads	☐	☐	☐
Old Bills	☐	☐	☐
Phone Books / Yellow Pages	☐	☐	☐
Receipts	☐	☐	☐
Rewards Cards	☐	☐	☐
Staple Remover	☐	☐	☐
Sticky Notes	☐	☐	☐

Stress Balls	☐	☐	☐
Trophies / Awards	☐	☐	☐

NOTES

1. (n.d.). Retrieved 2019, from https://conspicuousconsumption.org/
2. The Dharma Bums Quotes by Jack Kerouac. (n.d.). Retrieved 2019, from https://www.goodreads.com/work/quotes/827497
3. Bailey, N., & Bailey, N. (2016, December 21). Minimalism, Buddhism, and the ties between the two. Retrieved from https://medium.com/@njbailey/minimalism-buddhism-and-the-ties-between-the-two-1adac846aac0
4. Saxbe, D. E., & Repetti, R. (2009). No Place Like Home: Home Tours Correlate With Daily Patterns of Mood and Cortisol. *Personality and Social Psychology Bulletin,36*(1), 71-81. doi:10.1177/0146167209352864
5. (UCTV), U. O. (2013, October 30). Retrieved 2019, from https://www.youtube.com/watch?v=3AhSNsBs2Y0
6. Life at Home in the Twenty-First Century: 32 Families Open Their Doors. (2017, August 15). Retrieved from https://www.amazon.com/dp/1938770129/?tag=grs17-20
7. Neural pathway. (2019, April 06). Retrieved from https://en.wikipedia.org/wiki/Neural_pathway
8. (n.d.). Retrieved from http://www.human-memory.net/brain_neurons.html
9. Overcoming Destructive Habits with Neuroplasticity. (2016, June 15). Retrieved from https://balancedachievement.com/psychology/neuroplasticity/
10. Overcoming Destructive Habits with Neuroplasticity. (2016, June 15). Retrieved from https://balancedachievement.com/psychology/neuroplasticity/
11. Saruwatari, J. (2015, March 17). Behind the Clutter: Truth. Love. Meaning. Purpose. Retrieved from https://www.amazon.com/Behind-Clutter-Truth-Meaning-Purpose/dp/1614486166
12. Ewafa. (2017, December 13). Retrieved 2019, from https://www.youtube.com/watch?v=J54k7WrbfMg&feature=youtu.be
13. SPARTANLIFECOACH, R. G. (2018, November 18). Retrieved 2019, from https://www.youtube.com/watch?v=dmXcjvL9VSc&feature=youtu.be
14. Sam Vaknin. (2019, June 01). Retrieved from https://en.wikipedia.org/wiki/Sam_Vaknin
15. Seiter, C. (2019, January 18). The Psychology of Social Media: Why We Like, Comment, and Share Online. Retrieved from https://buffer.com/resources/psychology-of-social-media
16. Talks, T. (2017, June 22). Retrieved 2019, from https://www.youtube.com/watch?v=Czg_9C7gw0o&feature=youtu.be
17. Talks, T. (2016, September 19). Retrieved 2019, from https://www.youtube.com/watch?v=3E7hkPZ-HTk&feature=youtu.be
18. Jaffee, S. R., Hanscombe, K. B., Haworth, C. M., Davis, O. S., & Plomin, R. (2012). Chaotic Homes and Children's Disruptive Behavior. *Psychological Science,23*(6), 643-650. doi:10.1177/0956797611431693

19. Your Closets, Your Clutter, and Your Cognitions. (n.d.). Retrieved 2019, from https://www.google.com/amp/s/www.psychologytoday.com/us/blog/the-psychology-dress/201202/your-closets-your-clutter-and-your-cognitions-1?amp
20. Organic Facts. (2019, March 25). Health Benefits & Side Effects of Tulsi Tea. Retrieved from https://www.organicfacts.net/health-benefits/herbs-and-spices/tulsi-tea.html
21. Pure Fiji. (2016, March 21). The 5 Best Beauty Benefits of Coconut Oil. Retrieved 2019, from https://www.purefiji.com/blog/benefits-coconut-oil/
22. Shiffer, E. (2019, February 25). 4 Surprising Ways Apple Cider Vinegar Can Help Your Skin. Retrieved 2019, from https://www.menshealth.com/health/a25846878/apple-cider-vinegar-skin-benefits/
23. Muthoni, J. (2018, January 17). How lemon and honey can work wonders on your body. Retrieved 2019, from https://www.standardmedia.co.ke/evewoman/article/2001266250/how-lemon-and-honey-can-work-wonders-on-your-body
24. Spot, T. I. (2015, November 06). 5 AWESOME GRAPES FACE MASKS TO MAKE YOUR SKIN RADIANT. Retrieved from https://theindianspot.com/5-awesome-grapes-face-masks-to-make-your-skin-radiant/
25. Skincareox. (2019, March 13). 28 Best Organic & Natural Toners For Every Skin Type. Retrieved 2019, from https://www.skincareox.com/28-best-organic-natural-toners-for-every-skin-type/
26. Using Honey and Cinnamon for Acne. (n.d.). Retrieved 2019, from https://www.healthline.com/health/honey-and-cinnamon-for-acne
27. 10 Benefits of Golden (Turmeric) Milk and How to Make It. (n.d.). Retrieved 2019, from https://www.healthline.com/nutrition/golden-milk-turmeric
28. 7 Natural Face Packs Our Grandmothers Used for Beautiful Skin. (2018, April 30). Retrieved 2019, from https://food.ndtv.com/beauty/7-natural-face-packs-our-grandmothers-used-for-beautiful-skin-1684221
29. Martin, L. (2019, May 06). How to Make an Avocado Mask for Hair. Retrieved from https://www.wikihow.com/Make-an-Avocado-Mask-for-Hair
30. NatureHelps.Me. (2015, September 16). Miraculous Masks with Almond Oil for Face & Hair. Retrieved 2019, from https://naturehelps.me/natural-remedies/miraculous-masks-almond-oil-face-hair
31. Wennersten, K. (2013, May 3) Coconut Milk and Lemon Juice – The Perfect Hair Conditioning Treatment. Retrieved 2019, from https://coconutoilpost.com/ingredients/coconut-milk/coconut-milk-and-lemon-juice-the-perfect-hair-conditioning-treatment/
32. Rajapet, M., Choudhary, T., Choudhary, T., Rajapet, M., Rajapet, M., & Rajapet, M. (n.d.). Castor Oil For Hair Growth - How To Use It The Right Way? Retrieved from https://www.stylecraze.com/articles/castor-oil-for-hair-growth/
33. Egg Yolk & Olive Oil for Hair. (n.d.). Retrieved 2019, from https://www.livestrong.com/article/188279-egg-yolk-olive-oil-for-hair/
34. Why You Should Be Using A Vinegar Rinse. (n.d.). Retrieved from https://www.redken.com/blog/haircare/why-you-should-be-using-a-vinegar-rinse-for-hair
35. Rajapet, M. (n.d.). Henna For Hair: 9 Simple & Effective Hair Packs. Retrieved 2019, from https://www.stylecraze.com/articles/henna-for-hair/#gref

36. What Does Amla Powder Do for Your Hair? (n.d.). Retrieved 2019, from https://www.healthline.com/health/beauty-skin-care/amla-powder-for-hair
37. Shikakai Shampoo: Using Shikakai Powder to Wash Your Hair. (2019, May 26). Retrieved from https://www.curlcentric.com/shikakai-shampoo/
38. Compound Exercises: Benefits, 6 Examples, Safety Tips. (n.d.). Retrieved 2019, from https://www.healthline.com/health/fitness-exercise/compound-exercises
39. Craig, B., Brown, R., & Everhart, J. (1989). Effects of progressive resistance training on growth hormone and testosterone levels in young and elderly subjects. *Mechanisms of Ageing and Development,49*(2), 159-169. doi:10.1016/0047-6374(89)90099-7
40. Benefits of Isolation Exercise. (n.d.). Retrieved 2019, from https://www.ptonthenet.com/articles/Benefits-of-Isolation-Exercise-2620
41. Bodybuildingcom. (2018, March 19). What Is The Best HIIT Workout? Retrieved 2019, from https://www.bodybuilding.com/content/what-is-the-best-hiit-workout.html
42. (2015, April 02). Retrieved 2019, from https://www.peta.org/videos/meat-wastes-water/
43. Ofei, M. (2019, May 19). How a Plant-Based Lifestyle Can Help Your Health. Retrieved from https://theminimalistvegan.com/plant-based-lifestyle-health/
44. Arthur, M. (2016, August 01). The Body Was Designed to Heal Itself. Retrieved 2019, from http://www.healthinbalance.com/blog-1/2016/8/1/the-body-was-designed-to-health-itself
45. Week 2: Tune into Your Body's Wisdom. (2016, October 07). Retrieved from https://chopra.com/free-programs/awaken-to-happiness/week-2-tune-into-your-bodys-wisdom
46. Adaptogenic Herbs: What Are Adaptogens? (2016, February 25). Retrieved 2019, from https://www.globalhealingcenter.com/natural-health/what-are-adaptogens/
47. Li, N. P., & Kanazawa, S. (2016). Country roads, take me home… to my friends: How intelligence, population density, and friendship affect modern happiness. *British Journal of Psychology,107*(4), 675-697. doi:10.1111/bjop.12181
48. Mcmains, S., & Kastner, S. (2011). Interactions of Top-Down and Bottom-Up Mechanisms in Human Visual Cortex. *Journal of Neuroscience,31*(2), 587-597. doi:10.1523/jneurosci.3766-10.2011
49. Founded by Marie Kondo. (n.d.). Retrieved 2019, from https://konmari.com/
50. Sasaki, F. (2017, April 11). Goodbye, Things: The New Japanese Minimalism. Retrieved from https://www.amazon.com/Goodbye-Things-New-Japanese-Minimalism/dp/0393609030
51. Oppong, T. (2018, January 10). Ikigai: The Japanese Secret to a Long and Happy Life Might Just Help You Live a More Fulfilling... Retrieved from https://medium.com/thrive-global/ikigai-the-japanese-secret-to-a-long-and-happy-life-might-just-help-you-live-a-more-fulfilling-9871d01992b7
52. Wabi-sabi. (2019, June 10). Retrieved from https://en.wikipedia.org/wiki/Wabi-sabi
53. Your Closets, Your Clutter, and Your Cognitions. (n.d.). Retrieved from https://www.google.com/amp/s/www.psychologytoday.com/us/blog/the-psychology-dress/201202/your-closets-your-clutter-and-your-cognitions-1?amp

More books by Lola

A Morning Routine:

More Energetic, Productive,
Stress Free Days for Those with Normal Lives

Book and meditations available on

Amazon
https://amzn.to/2w5JzJ1

Audible
https://adbl.co/2IO5UmE

Want a Free Sleep Chart? Follow me as I write my way to a better life.
www.lolarmarie.com/sign-up

***Lola Ray Marie** loves to write, bathe in sun-rays and ponder the mysteries of life. She is also the author of "A Morning Routine" her debut Self-Help book.*

Follow Lola on Instagram @lola.r.marie